Sagittarius

23 November – 22 December

First published in Great Britain 2009
by Harlequin Mills & Boon Limited,
Eton House, 18-24 Paradise Road, Richmond, Surrey TW9 1SR

Copyright © Dadhichi Toth 2008 & 2009

ISBN: 978 0 263 87073 2

Typeset at Midland Typesetters Australia

Harlequin Mills & Boon policy is to use papers that are natural, renewable and recyclable products and made from wood grown in sustainable forests. The logging and manufacturing processes conform to the legal environmental regulations of the country of origin.

Printed and bound in Spain
by Litografia Rosés S.A., Barcelona

About
Dadhichi

Dadhichi is one of Australia's foremost astrologers. He has the ability to draw from complex astrological theory to provide clear, easily understandable advice and insights for people who want to know what their future might hold.

In the 26 years that Dadhichi has been practising astrology, face reading and other esoteric studies, he has conducted over 9,500 consultations. His clients include celebrities, political and diplomatic figures, and media and corporate identities from all over the world.

Dadhichi's unique blend of astrology and face reading helps people fulfil their true potential. His extensive experience practising western astrology is complemented by his research into the theory and practice of eastern systems of astrology.

Dadhichi features in numerous newspapers and magazines and he also appears regularly on many of Australia's leading television and radio networks, where many of his political and worldwide forecasts have proved uncannily accurate.

His website www.astrology.com.au is now one of the top ten online Australian lifestyle sites and, in conjunction with www.facereader.com, www.soulconnector.com and www.psychjuice.com, they attract over half a million visitors monthly. The websites offer a wide variety of features, helpful information and personal services.

Dedicated to The Light of Intuition
Sri V. Krishnaswamy—mentor and friend
With thanks to Julie, Joram, Isaac and Janelle

Welcome from
Dadhichi

Dear Friend,

Welcome! It's great to have you here, reading your horoscope, trying to learn more about yourself and what's in store for you in 2010.

I visited Mexico a while ago and stumbled upon the Mayan prophecies for 2012, which, they say, is the year when the longstanding calendar we use in the western world supposedly stops! If taken literally, some people could indeed believe that 'the end of the world is near'. However, I see it differently.

Yes, it might seem as though the world is getting harder and harder to deal with, especially when fear enters our lives. But, I believe that 'the end' indicated by these Mayan prophecies has more to do with the end that will create new beginnings for our societies, more to do with making changes to our material view of life and some necessary adjustments for the human race to progress and prosper in future. So let's get one thing straight: you and I will both be around after 2012, reading our 2013 horoscopes!

My prediction and advice centres around keeping a cool mind and not reacting to the fear that could overtake us. Of course, this isn't easy, especially when media messages might increase our anxiety about such things as the impacts of global warming or the scarcity of fossil fuels.

I want you to understand that it is certainly important to be aware and play your part in making the world a better place; however, the best and surest way to support global goals is to help yourself first. Let me explain. If everyone focused just a little more on improving *themselves* rather than just pointing their finger to criticise others, it would result in a dramatic change and improvement; not just globally, but societally. And, of course, you mustn't forget what a positive impact this would have on your personal relationships as well.

Astrology focuses on self-awareness; your own insights into your personality, thinking processes and relationships. This is why this small book you have in your hand doesn't only concentrate on what is going to happen, but more importantly how you can *make* things happen positively through being your best.

I have always said that there are two types of people: puppets and actors. The first simply react to each outside stimulus and are therefore slaves of their environment, and even of their own minds and emotions. They are puppets in the hands of karma. The other group I call actors. Although they can't control what happens to them all the time, either, they are better able to adapt and gain something purposeful in their lives. They are in no way victims of circumstance.

I hope you will use what is said in the following pages to become the master of your destiny, and not rely on the predictions that are given as mere fate but as valuable guidelines to use intelligently when life presents you with its certain challenges.

Neither the outside world, nor the ups and downs that occur in your life, should affect your innermost spirituality and self-confidence. Take control: look beyond your current challenges and use them as the building blocks of experience to create success and fulfilment in the coming year.

I believe you have the power to become great and shine your light for all to see. I hope your 2010 horoscope book will be a helpful guide and inspiration for you.

Warm regards, and may the stars shine brightly for you in 2010!

Your Astrologer,

Dadhichi Toth

Contents

The Sagittarius
Identity

Too low they build who build beneath the stars.

—Edward Young

Sagittarius: A Snapshot

Key Characteristics

Magnanimous, honest, expansive, generous, reckless, extroverted, proud, larger than life and free

Compatible Star Signs

Aries, Leo, Libra, Aquarius

Key Life Phrase

I expand

Life Goals

To explore the world and grow in understanding

Platinum Assets

Fearlessness, optimism and goodwill

Zodiac Totem

The Centaur

Zodiac Symbol

♐

Zodiac Facts

Ninth sign of the zodiac; mutable, barren, masculine, dry

Element

Fire

Famous Sagittarians

Sir Winston Churchill, Ludwig van Beethoven,
Mark Twain, Francis Albert Sinatra, Jim Morrison,
Sonia Gandhi, Walt Disney, Jane Austen,
John F. Kennedy Jr, Tina Turner, Tyra Banks, Judi Dench,
Bruce Lee, Jimi Hendrix, Woody Allen,
Samuel L. Jackson, Sinead O'Connor, Britney Spears

Sagittarius: Your profile

The centaur is an excellent totem that truly represents the Sagittarian personality. Being half man and half horse, it reveals your dual nature and your ability to enjoy the better of two worlds—that of humanity and also that of a more primal nature. Incidentally, the human portion of the centaur is aiming an arrow to the heavens, indicating your far-reaching visions and aspirations.

The human part of your personality shows your generous and easygoing nature. You view life with great optimism and others find this part of your character absolutely infectious. People love being around you and feel uplifted by your warm and consistent enthusiasm.

You are ruled by Jupiter, the luckiest of planets, which means many Sagittarians don't have to try too hard for life to bring them many opportunities, great friends and spiritual wealth. Interestingly, Jupiter used to be known by the name Jove, from which the word 'jovial' is derived. Need I say more? Sagittarians are full of laughter, constantly joking and remaining positive, even in the midst of difficult times.

You are self-confident to the point that, at times, others might even consider you a little over the top in your optimism. You never take 'no' for an answer and also rarely believe things will go wrong. The funny thing is, usually you are successful and do land on your feet, even if times are tough. It's probably because your philosophy is that positive thinking is the solution.

You can't understand how being down on yourself, complaining, or seeing things in a negative light will improve things in any way. And you like to share this philosophy with others. Part of your nature is to see to it that others operate at their best and, if you can help lift their spirits to show them an alternative way of living, this gives you great satisfaction.

In your desire to become great, to achieve wonderful things in life, you do have a tendency to overstep the mark and many Sagittarians are quite excessive in everything they do. You must be careful not to let your zealous nature overlook the most important catchphrase for Sagittarius, which is 'moderation'. By balancing your far-sighted goals and ambitions with a moderate lifestyle, and keeping in mind the limitations of others who have to live with you, you will be successful and happy as well.

Sagittarians seem to know how to be at the right place at the right time. This is called luck. You have the knack of attracting the right people and public circumstances to give you windows of opportunity that others can only dream about. And this is not just about money. You are keenly interested in becoming a better person. Using your personal growth and self-understanding is a way of improving the world and your loved ones, as well as yourself.

It would be safe to say that as a Sagittarian you have itchy feet. You don't like staying still because you understand just how much there is to learn about and explore in the world. You are an adventurer by nature and from an early age will have wanted to seek out different cultures, unusual people and experiences that can give meaning to your life. You like the idea of travelling and you feel connected to 'the whole'. The world is your playground.

You never sit still and can get rather bored if life is not as stimulating as you would like it to be. You don't have a large circle of friends, but if they do become a little boring, you have no hesitation in moving on, because you understand that life is all too short and you need to extract the most out of it. This is not to say you use people, but you are fully aware of the importance of connecting with those whom you can share mutual interests.

For you, Sagittarius, there are no limits. A limit is something that the mind places upon itself. You have an intimate understanding that the mind can create anything at once, which includes good and bad things. You get quite frustrated with people who are negative and self-limiting. If you perceive that there's no way of helping them, you quickly exit the scene, focusing your attention on those whom you feel will appreciate what you have to offer them.

Sagittarians are extremely intuitive and spiritual, which is because your ruling planet Jupiter has the ability to give you great foresight. You understand without thought. You have a keen sense of whether or not someone is a good person. Strangely this doesn't stop you from generously giving of yourself, even to those who could hurt you. Sooner or later you will learn that you must pick your mark or your magnanimous nature will start to work against your best interests.

Three classes of Sagittarius

If you were born between the 23rd of November and the 2nd of December you are a true Sagittarian at heart and will fully display all of these Sagittarian characteristics. You are particularly adventurous by nature and have an up-beat personality, which will assure you of success. Yours will be a life full of adventure, luck and wonderful friends.

If your birth date falls between the 3rd of December and the 12th of December, hot and active Mars also plays a part in your life, making you a rather temperamental individual. You are active, restless and sometimes a little bit impatient. Playing sport will be an ideal way for you to vent your spleen and balance your personality.

If you were born between the 13th and the 22nd of December, the Sun and Leo colour your temperament considerably. This is a lucky omen for you and makes you bright, successful and magnetic in personality. There's nothing much you won't achieve in life, which indicates the presence of good karma that will make you successful.

Sagittarius role model: Sir Winston Churchill

Sir Winston Churchill displays many of the Sagittarian traits mentioned above. Idealistic and capable, he was an inspiring leader who was always concerned with the greater good. Due to his clear foresight and excellent decision-making skills, the British and their Allies were inspired towards success during the Second World War. He is considered one of the greatest leaders in history and, of course, holds before you the true Sagittarian ideal.

Sagittarius: The light side

You never take 'no' for an answer, even if others tell you something can't be done. Being the supreme optimist, you get cracking on what you believe is a worthwhile project or path in life, even when you know the obstacles can be almost insurmountable. You love a challenge, which could be one of the reasons why you attempt what others consider to be impossible. In the process you show others how it can be done—with energy, persistence and a wonderful light-hearted optimism.

You don't believe there are problems in life, only opportunities for self-improvement. You truly do accept the fact that, out of something bad, something good can arise. Some of your friends and family find this a little hard to reconcile. Not everyone can think on such a lofty level. Try to be patient with them if you are persuading them to adopt your philosophy.

You have an amazing ability to compete and will always be a fair sport. You do not believe you must crush your competitor, only to play the game as hard and as fair as you can. You're impartial, a good judge and a wonderful friend. You are loyal to those who support you and can even forgive your enemies, which is something most people find impossible to do.

You're the consummate dreamer and your ambitions are larger and harder to achieve than most, but you don't see the point of aiming for mediocrity. You'd rather achieve something grand and then print your name on it for posterity's sake.

You're a great competitor in life, playing seriously and honestly. However, as with all fire signs, you would always prefer to win. If on occasion you do lose, you enjoy the thrill of the game regardless. Your fair-mindedness is probably one of your best traits.

Sagittarius: The shadow side

Because you exhibit such a positive energy and believe so much in yourself, you have a tendency to take things to the extreme, never believing that you can fail. I don't want to clip your wings, but there comes a time when you must examine yourself impartially and accept that we do have limitations, being human.

Try to listen to others' viewpoints if they have the expertise, wisdom and experience to prove to you that your approach may not be completely correct. You could have an over-inflated sense of your own opinion, which makes you appear egotistical to others.

Your belief about yourself can at times also extend to your political, religious and social ideas, which you vehemently defend and try to force down other people's throats. Try to show others the same respect that you wish to have shown to you.

It's not a good idea for Sagittarians to gamble. You may have a compulsive streak, which indicates you need to control any obsessive tendencies. Learn to develop balance and steadiness in your life.

Sagittarius woman

Sagittarian women are such a lot of fun! With women born under this sign, life is always exciting, up-beat and interesting.

If you're a Sagittarian woman and are reading this, you'll appreciate what I mean when I refer to you as a bomb waiting to go off! You hate being bored and will see to it that your life is full of activities, social interaction, travels and many diverse ambitions to keep your mind busy and engaged.

However, you never allow these enjoyable activities to interfere with your principled approach to life as a whole. You have a high degree of integrity, always relying on honesty to put forward your point. When dealing with others, they know quite well that a Sagittarian woman doesn't beat around the bush and calls a situation as it is. Because of this you are well respected among your peers and in your work.

You can't overlook the good in life and in people, even when others have given up on certain individuals. You don't believe that it's impossible to extract the best out of others, so this makes you a wonderful leader, carer and helper. Even if you don't pursue teaching as a profession, there's something about your life that is in itself an example to others—a model of how to live and enjoy, how to love and share. These are Sagittarian ideals.

When I speak to people and ask them what they feel is the most attractive aspect of someone's personality, it usually isn't a person's good looks. It is always how intelligent and humorous another individual is. This is why a Sagittarian female may be just so enticing to prospective partners. Her enthusiasm and unique personality is irresistible.

Some people find you a little intimidating because your energy is just so strong. When you're in the company of others who don't have the same level of self-confidence and self-determination, you may need to tone it down just a little. If you are a less developed Sagittarian woman, you might be somewhat self-centred, running roughshod over others' sensitivities. If this happens, it could be time to re-evaluate your approach, don't you think?

You'll have to expect your fair share of envy on your life path because other women don't feel all that comfortable about you stealing the limelight all the time. You are a bright star among social circles, which can set other less confident people against you. Because you have a deep and clear intuitive power, you'll understand who these enemies are. My suggestion is that you're better off avoiding them. If you try hard to win them over, you probably won't be successful 100 per cent of the time.

You like to be involved in activities that make a difference to the world. You'll have a large circle of acquaintances and some of them will also be well connected. You will utilise your networks not only for social good but for humanitarian purposes as well.

You have a fiery and creative mind and need to find activities to fulfil this part of your being. Even if your work is not considered a particularly creative line of endeavour, you like to find ways to make the work interesting and as creative as possible. You have a knack for doing this, and it is quite amazing how you can turn the mundane into the extraordinary. You like to involve every part of your being in what you do.

Not many people have the ability to laugh at themselves, but you don't believe it is of any benefit to take yourself too seriously, do you, Sagittarius? Fortunately you've come to realise that in this world life will be a much easier journey if you lighten it with laughter, and spread that light all around.

Sagittarius man

Sagittarian men are dynamos of energy, passion and action. If you're born under this star sign then you are fortunate to be born with such abundant enthusiasm, which is the result of fiery and noble Jupiter in your life. Jupiter is your ruling planet, which makes you confident under all circumstances and constantly concerned with how to improve not only your own life but the lives of others. You hate the thought of being successful at the expense of other people. That is, if you're born with the nobler traits of Sagittarius.

You are a born leader and this is because you're able to steer people in a direction that brings out the best in them. You've learned to do this in yourself and don't easily feel defeated, even under the most trying of circumstances. You can't handle the idea of being defeated or losing in competition. If—and I say 'if' with a capital I and a capital F—you do lose, you are gracious with it. You're a good sportsman and, even when the chips are down, you nevertheless give 100 per cent of yourself if you decide on a path of action. This is inspiring to the 'troops', so to speak, whether they are work colleagues or family members.

In life you are idealistic and aim for the stars. You don't believe there's any point in doing something half-heartedly. Your attitude is that, if you have to spend time with someone or on something, then it may as well be done properly.

Sagittarius men have the incredible ability of spinning a wonderful yarn. You love sharing stories of your experiences with others and they are inspired by these anecdotal instances. At times, however, even though you are able to captivate your audience, you do have a tendency to exaggerate a little so as to embellish your account to make you more endearing to others.

Try not to promise things you can't deliver, Sagittarius. You don't like letting others down but, in your enthusiasm, in the heat of the moment, you are likely to give assurances that on second thoughts you may not be able to keep. Always have a diary handy and be straightforward with others if you can't quite do what they ask of you. They will appreciate your honesty in saying so.

Competition is very important to you and will rank very high on your list of priorities. Sagittarian men are usually very good at sports and may even participate in professional arenas to satisfy their competitive urges. Sports including tennis, cricket, golf and football give you the opportunity to express your determination and the high level of energy you possess. The more competitive a sport, the better for you. As a Sagittarian you have no problem pushing yourself to the limits and love nothing more than a great win.

Because of your strong belief system, you have a tendency to put everything on the line. This can be seen in your relationships, your business, or simply a goal you have in mind. However, pace yourself, because many Sagittarians overestimate their abilities. Take the time to understand your subject and to enjoy the journey rather than working wholly and solely for the end goal.

You have a wonderful ability to communicate and can convey your concepts and vision in a unique manner, unlike many of the other star signs. You are also very impartial in the way you deal with people. It doesn't matter whether you are dealing with a merchant banker or a farmer. Your compassionate nature and equal mindedness will see to it that you never look down on anyone.

As a husband and father you'll bring a lot of joy to your family and can be a great role model to your children. Actually, many Sagittarian men never cease to be big kids at heart themselves!

Sagittarius child

Your Sagittarian child is boisterous, adventurous and full of laughter. Even when they are naughty, it's hard not to love them because of that cheeky attitude they tend to exude to deflect their misdeeds. You know this is true, but can't help yourself because they are such loving beings!

You need to have lots of space for a Sagittarian and hopefully your house has a large garden with many outdoor activities at hand. The Sagittarian individual is born under the element of fire and therefore is creative, physically active and by no means a housebound kid.

If you've been a bit of a couch potato prior to giving birth to a Sagittarian child, that will all change drastically the moment your child is old enough to walk. They'll be out and about ... and make sure you have a leash because they are kids on a mission when it comes to exploring the local terrain. This is one of the signature characteristics of Sagittarius—adventure.

Your Sagittarian child is especially generous with time, money and other resources. They will want to share their toys but will be baffled when other more selfish children don't act in the same way to reciprocate their kindness. You may have a job explaining to them the ways of the world. This will disappoint them because it is so foreign to their beautiful little personalities. But it's a good idea to do it, because the real world is indeed one in which most people don't want to extend generosity the way a Sagittarian child does.

An excellent way of directing your child's energies if they are born under the sign of the centaur is to get them into sport, and lots of it. This child will need more than the usual dose of running and competitive activities to keep them calm and focused on their other duties such as schoolwork and homework. Make them sweat, even if they are girls. Girls born under Sagittarius are no less active or adventurous than boys, believe me.

When your Sagittarian child doesn't come out a winner, you need to teach them the graceful art of losing with a smile. This may take time but with practice they will learn to be great sportspeople and not feel that winning is everything. Teach them these important guidelines because it will help them not only in their sporting activities but in their life as a whole.

Romance, love and marriage

In the first part of the Sagittarian identity reading, I mentioned the fact that the centaur is half human and half horse. I spoke of the fact that Sagittarius is a humanitarian sign, but that it is also just as equally concerned with the primal and sensual aspects of life.

Sagittarius, you are attracted to people and will spend much of your time trying to find the partner who will fulfil your needs and reciprocate your generosity, affection and spiritual ideals as well.

One of the most important aspects or character-istics you look for in someone is that of intelligence and good humour. Yes, you are passionate in the physical sense, but by the same token don't believe that passion is the be-all and end-all of romance, love and marriage. Your inclination is to want to deepen your bond with someone if they can first show you they have a human side and are willing to share it with you.

You enjoy good company and will give so much to the one whom you choose as your soulmate. You give your body, mind and soul to your lover, and expect the same in return. But you enjoy your freedom as well, which may be difficult for some of the other star signs. You hate being caged in, controlled or interrogated too much about your activities. You believe in giving your partner the same freedom that you demand. Because this may be a struggle for other star signs to understand, you should consider carefully who it is you want to spend the rest of your life with.

When a Sagittarian gives their love, they will still expect to have the freedom to pursue their intellectual and spiritual objectives without any interference. You'll soon learn quickly that the Sagittarian will do an aboutface on the relationship if you try to curtail their liberties in any way.

In the bedroom, the Sagittarian is an excellent lover. They are infused with the element of fire, which rules them. Passion, demonstrativeness and a high degree of energy means that Sagittarians perform best when they are with partners of equal calibre. Not only that, Sagittarians love excess, so this is not a matter of intimacy once or twice a week, but once or twice a day! I suggest that, if you don't have the appetite for long, loving, sensual sessions of lovemaking, do not apply for a long-term relationship with a Sagittarian.

In the early stages of life some Sagittarians tend to want to test their prowess and see just how many people they can attract to them. This is more the case with men but some of the female centaurs are of the same temperament. Your passion certainly needs fulfilling and it's best to do this before you give a commitment to the one with whom you wish to share your life.

Venus strongly influences your friendships and social life. Choosing the best in culture, fashion and style is all part of your Sagittarian make-up and will also have a sway in the type of friends and partners you choose. You want someone who has class and elegance. Although you are happy-go-lucky and even tempered, you still need someone in your life who is a reasonably refined individual.

Health, wellbeing and diet

Sagittarians usually enjoy good health. Endorphins, the healing chemicals in our bodies, are produced when we are happy, so your up-beat attitude is a positive benefit for you physically. Your ruling planet Jupiter ensures you will live long and be strong, but try to control some of your excessive traits. Disease and other physical problems are caused by overeating and pushing yourself too hard.

Exercise and sport are a natural turn on for most Sagittarians, so you have a shot at good health by giving free rein to your love of the outdoors, physical mobility, and generally enjoying the air and sun, not to mention the ocean.

This optimistic mental attitude will bring you good luck and wonderful health right into your old age and, as with most of us, if you do happen to have the odd physical problem, you have remarkable recuperative powers, so don't worry.

Sagittarius has rulership over the thighs and hip areas, which include the pelvis and lower back. Constitutionally these are weak points. Because Taurus also regulates the health of Sagittarius, your neck, throat and upper shoulders can also give you the occasional bit of trouble. Regular massages and yoga will help keep these parts of your body flexible and in good working condition.

Food can become a problem for some Sagittarians who have a tendency to gain weight with age. This reflects a lack of willpower when it comes to rich foods and fine dining. You should eat smaller meals more regularly, and of course try to burn off those excess calories through exercise.

The old adage, 'eat like a king in the morning, a prince at lunch, and a pauper at night' is the saying all Sagittarians should commit to memory and apply to their dietary habits. Stay away from high-carbohydrate foods, particularly later in the day and into the night. As your metabolism slows down at this time, you are less able to digest any remaining food quickly.

The best foods for Sagittarius are lentils, broccoli, olives and the greener leafy vegetables. These have all the nutrients, vitamins and minerals your body needs. If you must eat meat, try to avoid high-fat meats and excessively processed foods like salami. Jupiter regulates the liver and this indicates that some Sagittarians may have a problem processing some of these highly refined foods.

Work

People might be forgiven for feeling that many Sagittarians don't seem to be that driven or ambitious due to their carefree and easygoing nature. But this is not the case. In fact, many hardworking and successful individuals are born under the sign of Sagittarius. The sign of Virgo has much to do with the professional aptitude and precision of your career path, given that it rules your zone of employment. You're talented in both detailed and 'big picture' work.

You're extremely skilful at what you do and never take 'no' for an answer. You like to be successful on a grand scale. Be careful, though, because many Sagittarians also have a tendency to overwork. Some have been known to become workaholics, selling their souls for the sake of some professional and financial success, much to the detriment of their personal and family lives. Again, as always, one of the main key words for Sagittarius is moderation.

You generate tremendous amounts of enthusiasm in every aspect of your work. Such areas as sales and presentation-style industries such as teaching and corporate or executive training are ideal arenas in which Sagittarians can display their many personable skills.

Jupiter also gives you an ability to work in the banking and financial industries. Law, foreign relations or the import–export business, or travel and cultural professions have an appeal for you as well.

Because of your love of independence, an entrepreneurial job would ideally suit you and give you the independence you so desire.

Key to karma, spirituality and emotional balance

The Sagittarius key words are 'I expand', and the challenge for you in this lifetime is to balance your warm and generous nature with control. You can still aim for those big goals, but try not to go beyond your limits.

In your past life you were headstrong and your ego was very powerful. This time around you will be learning the lesson of humility. Try to listen to others' spiritual and religious viewpoints even if you think you know better. Sagittarians like to take things to extremes but curbing your excesses is another important life lesson which will assist you in attaining your material and spiritual goals. Discipline yourself and moderate all aspects of your lifestyle for optimum results.

Your lucky days

Your luckiest days are Monday, Tuesday, Thursday and Sunday.

Your lucky numbers

Remember that the forecasts given later in the book will help you optimise your chances of winning. Your lucky numbers are:

1, 10, 19, 28, 37, 46

3, 12, 21, 30, 39, 48

9, 18, 27, 36, 45, 54

Your destiny years

Your most important years are 3, 12, 21, 30, 39, 48, 57, 66, 75 and 84.

SAGITTARIUS

Star Sign
Compatibility

*No man is truly married until he understands every
word his wife is NOT saying.*

—Unknown

Romantic compatibility

How compatible are you with your current partner,
lover or friend? Did you know that astrology can
reveal a whole new level of understanding between
people simply by looking at their star sign and that
of their partner? In this chapter I'd like to share
some special insights that will help you better
appreciate your strengths and challenges using Sun
sign compatibility.

The Sun reflects your drive, willpower and
personality. The essential qualities of two star signs
blend like two pure colours, producing an entirely
new colour. Relationships, similarly, produce their
own emotional colours when two people interact.
The following is a general guide to your romantic
prospects with others and how, by knowing the
astrological 'colour' of each other, the art of love
can help you create a masterpiece.

When reading the following I ask you to remember
that no two star signs are ever *totally* incompatible.
With effort and compromise, even the most 'difficult' astrological matches can work. Don't close
your mind to the full range of life's possibilities!
Learning about each other and ourselves is the
most important facet of astrology.

Quick-reference guide: Horoscope compatibility between signs (percentage)

	Aries	Taurus	Gemini	Cancer	Leo	Virgo	Libra	Scorpio	Sagittarius	Capricorn	Aquarius	Pisces
Pisces	65	85	50	90	75	70	50	95	75	85	55	80
Aquarius	55	80	90	70	70	50	95	60	60	70	80	55
Capricorn	50	95	50	45	45	95	85	65	55	85	70	85
Sagittarius	90	50	75	55	95	70	80	80	85	55	60	75
Scorpio	80	85	60	95	75	85	85	90	85	65	60	95
Libra	70	75	90	60	65	80	80	85	80	85	95	50
Virgo	45	90	75	75	75	70	80	85	70	95	50	70
Leo	90	70	80	70	85	75	65	75	95	45	70	75
Cancer	65	80	60	75	70	75	60	95	55	45	70	90
Gemini	65	70	75	60	80	75	90	60	75	50	90	50
Taurus	65	70	70	80	70	90	75	85	60	95	80	85
Aries	60	70	70	65	90	45	70	80	90	50	55	65

Each star sign combination is followed by the elements of those star signs and the result of their combining. For instance, Aries is a fire sign and Aquarius is an air sign and this combination produces a lot of 'hot air'. Air feeds fire and fire warms air. In fact, fire requires air. However, not all air and fire combinations work. I have included information about the different birth periods within each star sign and this will throw even more light on your prospects for a fulfilling love life with any star sign you choose.

Good luck in your search for love, and may the stars shine upon you in 2010!

Compatibility quick-reference guide

Each of the twelve star signs has a greater or lesser affinity with one another. The quick-reference guide will show you who's hot and who's not so hot as far as your relationships are concerned.

SAGITTARIUS + ARIES
Fire + Fire = Explosion

This is a great blending of astrological elements; that is, fire with fire. Therefore, a relationship together is likely to be quite successful.

Both of you are born under outgoing star signs, which means you are sociable and love people. As well, you are both creative and spontaneous and therefore are interested in exploring life together and discovering what it has to offer.

Being adventurous fire signs, you and Aries desire to journey the world and learn about new things. Here is a fun combination for this one reason alone. Aries will keep you on your toes, and what you also like about them is the fact they are impulsive and sometimes a little capricious. This gives you a feeling that Aries will be able to meet your need for a sense of adventure and a constant element of surprise.

Aries can be inspiring with their high levels of energy. You have vision and they have drive, so this is a great mix that will motivate you not only romantically but in a business or creative venture as well.

The fire signs are very physically driven, therefore you are vital, energetic and love to challenge each other, yet inspire each other as well. You both work, play and live hard but can expect an enjoyable life as companions. Travelling together is quite likely because culture and variety are important to your lifestyles.

Passionate and sexual describes your relationship, but Aries is a little more temperamental, impulsive and irritable. You'll have to get used to dealing with these aspects of their characters.

Although Aries is usually quite argumentative, you aren't. Therefore this could leave Aries a little frustrated when you brush over their reactive responses.

There are a group of Arians born between the 31st of March and the 10th of April, and you have a really great rapport with these people. If you work at it, this could be a long-term relationship because you have the ability to intuit exactly what the other is feeling. It's quite a psychic relationship.

Another class of Aries is born between the 11th and the 20th of April. This too is a very good match for you. These are not your typical gung-ho Aries and will make you feel much more grounded than you're accustomed to. Your relationship will also be exciting, full of the enjoyment of a warm companionship together. You can expect to have many special engagements with them, and the two of you will naturally attract people to you.

The fire plus fire combination equals a red-hot relationship with Aries born between the 21st and the 30th of March. This particular mix works well because you are both ruled by Mars, which is the ruler of Aries. Mars sub-rules you along with the planet Jupiter. This could be anexplosive but also a very loving and passionate relationship.

SAGITTARIUS + TAURUS
Fire + Earth = Lava

You have an intense love of freedom, being born under the star sign of Sagittarius. But Taurus is a passive type, which will annoy you. They are not as prone to getting out and about and prefer the tried and tested, what you'd call a slightly boring comfort zone.

Taureans are jealous, possessive individuals, and this is not something you will tolerate, loving your freedom as much as you do. You need to feel independent and supported in your desire to grow and explore as much of life as possible.

Financially, Taurus needs to have more and more. They're extremely security conscious, and although you too have an expansive view of life and would like to be successful, it appears you are not as preoccupied with money as your Taurean partner is. In fact, money does tend to slip through your fingers and this will be a point that Taurus constantly raises with you, much to your chagrin.

The fire and earth signs are not totally complementary elements. You are attracted to each other, but the relationship may not be all that long lasting. You will need to find ways to draw the best out of each other to make this a durable match.

Taureans are especially inflexible in their opinions. You like to keep an open mind on all matters, even if you don't agree with someone else. Taurus is very different in this respect. You will become very irritated by their stubborn position.

Sagittarius and Taurus can be very lucky materially, but to you money is not all that counts. You'd like to think you can develop a deeper, more meaningful relationship with them.

Although your ruling planets are not particularly friendly, there is something to be said for your intimacy together. Taurus is a sensitive and caring sign and will tend to your needs, even if you're not particularly compatible on all the other issues discussed.

Taurus also has a need for strong family and a settled life, so you must be prepared to sacrifice some of the independence you're so accustomed to.

Those Taureans born between the 21st and the 29th of April are not at all compatible with Sagittarius. There is an increased influence of Venus, which means that health matters for you are adversely affected. They can be demanding, pushy individuals who make you feel rather frustrated.

There's a good rapport with Taureans born between the 30th of April and the 10th of May. They have an intellectual approach to life and therefore communication between the two of you will be enjoyable. This relationship, due to this strong point, has a good chance of going the distance.

Taureans are excellent money managers and therefore finance will be an important element of your relationship with them, but more so with those born between the 11th and the 21st of May. They are partially influenced by Saturn and the sign of Capricorn, so they are the most practical of the Taureans. If you're interested in financial ambitions of a professional nature, then your time together will be very much about making this a priority.

SAGITTARIUS + GEMINI
Fire + Air = Hot Air

This is an extremely stimulating combination, mainly because opposite signs such as yours attract, and attract strongly! Your elements are also quite compatible, yours being fire and Gemini being air. This indicates that there's considerable intellectual compatibility present due to the creative interaction between you. If you can develop on this one point—that is, the intellectual compatibility between you—your sexual life will also naturally flow and become extremely positive.

Even though both Sagittarius and Gemini are restless by nature, you do enjoy the variety that this gives you. I'd have to say you can always expect excitement and variety with them, too, so there'll never be a dull moment with your Gemini partner.

In matters of intimacy you are both very well suited as long as you talk together and take an interest in each other's intellectual and spiritual viewpoints. This will make you feel more open and loving with each other. Your intimate relationship with a Gemini is excellent because they are a creative sign. You'll be attracted to their very artful manner in the bedroom. Air and fire naturally warm and accentuate each other's qualities and so there will be a lot of sensual and emotional exchange between you, leading to an exciting physical relationship.

Although this is not the most idyllic match, it's still strong enough to keep you both interested and, as long as you're prepared to work at it, as is necessary for any relationship, you've got a chance for finding fulfilment with a Gemini partner.

You'll have an immediate attraction to any Gemini born between the 22nd of May and the 1st of June. You basically connect with them mentally, physically and emotionally. Each of you will feel your desires fulfilled by the other, which is because you resonate with each other socially and on a day-to-day basis.

With Geminis born between the 2nd and the 12th of June, you find it difficult to connect with their personalities. This bunch of Geminis is rather contradictory in nature, so why not first get to know them on the level of friendship before getting too involved? Once you feel more comfortable with each other, a deeper, more lasting relationship is likely to take place. The main thing here is to strengthen your ties of friendship together.

Highly strung Gemini individuals are born between the 13th and the 21st of June and, while you might feel really attracted to them, their disposition could affect your nerves and your peace of mind. You'll respect their mental capabilities, and you'll note that their intuition is very strong as well.

Coupled with their wonderful sense of humour and child-like innocence, you'll never be bored or lacking in fun times with them. These Gemini-born individuals have a tendency to say 'yes' to too many people, which keeps them constantly on their toes. If you like a busy lifestyle, then this is the relationship for you.

SAGITTARIUS + CANCER

Fire + Water = Steam

Cancer could be regarded as a complicated water sign and for that one reason they may hold you back in your estimation of them.

Although your ruling planets Jupiter and the Moon are friendly with each other, your temperaments are quite different. Therefore, if you choose to dance to the tune of life with a Cancer, you'll sometimes feel as though you're out of step with each other. Might I even say that one of you might start treading on the other's toes?

Cancer is a rather moody, temperamental type, being ruled by the ever-changing Moon. If you start spending large amounts of time in trying to handle this side of their personality, you might start to lose interest. Cancerians absorb much of the feelings in the air of the environment around them. Unfortunately your up-beat temperament may not be enough to keep them out of their pendulum-like mood swings.

Sagittarius, you are a very easygoing type and of course you love your independence. You'd hate to think anyone is going to take that away from you: 'No way, José!' But Cancer, who is for the most part a homebody, will want to clip your wings, making you feel quite suppressed. You won't stand for this, so it could be the downfall of a relationship between you.

Cancer is a domestic sign, naturally attracted to family and home life. They will need to know that you too want to have a family and have a genuine desire to support them in this goal. You must be prepared to give concessions in this respect and spend time with family. Or, if you're not that way inclined just yet, to show Cancer you are indeed willing to learn the ropes and be part of the group.

In issues of sexuality you will find that Cancer is very receptive and responsive to your needs, but you could be a little too excessive for their liking. And, having to tone things down is also not part of the Sagittarian temperament. Cancer is one of the most sensual zodiac signs, so it's quite likely a significant amount of passion will be sparked in your relationship with them. Remember, Cancer is an emotional sign and will never stand for any physicality of a harsh nature.

Life is a bit of a roller-coaster ride with Cancers born between the 22nd of June and the 3rd of July. We've already mentioned just how sensitive Cancer can be, but these individuals could be considered hypersensitive and you'll be constantly adjusting yourself to them. You'll need to curb your extravagant gestures because they will make them feel uneasy. They have a practical streak to their nature that is sometimes a little too straight and serious for your liking.

You're naturally attracted to Cancerians born between the 4th and the 13th of July, but it's best not to rush them too quickly and in too dramatic a fashion, or you might scare them away. Your family history, issues of culture and your philosophical viewpoints could be a challenge for both of you. Before the relationship becomes more serious you may need to sort out these aspects of your lives.

You feel comfortable with Cancers born between the 14th and the 23rd of July. Life with them should be quite satisfactory if you take the step and make the commitment with them.

SAGITTARIUS + LEO
Fire + Fire = Explosion

One would have to say that a relationship with Leo could be one of the most perfect matches under the zodiac for you. The fire signs resonate so well with each other that they always seem to click and get on so well. Mentally and emotionally you have a great chance of success with a Leo partner.

It doesn't bother you that Leo is so proud and sometimes even obstinate because your flexibility is a wonderful counterbalance to their proud and sometimes egotistical ways. You simply know how to balance each other so well.

There is something faithful about your relationship with Leo. The position of this zodiac sign indicates some past karma that you'll immediately recognise in each other when you meet. Leo is therefore a great mentor and you'll be constantly learning things from them.

Socially you are compatible and make a great impact wherever you go as a couple. You appreciate the fact that Leo is socially as enthusiastic and energetic as you are in making friends and sharing your experiences as a couple.

Passion is part of their nature and, although you are more easygoing than your Leo partner, the intuitive understanding between you seems to be a bridge that can lessen the gap between any differences you might have. Sexually you ignite each other's fires of passion and, being creative, you are both warm and demonstrative towards each other. There's nothing much lacking in the bedroom here!

When it comes to family life and a long-term relationship, you'll note that Leo is loyal. However, you do need to show them the same level of fidelity if the relationship is to last.

Your destiny intertwines wonderfully with Leos born between the 24th of July and the 4th of August, and this is because the Sun and Leo have much to do with your ideas of higher learning. Initially you may be physically attracted to these individuals when you first meet, but your relationship will soon grow into a beautiful, spiritual connection as well.

With Leos born between the 5th and the 14th of August, you see so much of yourself in them that it can be a little unsettling. Your character is highly visible in that you are both optimistic, outgoing and social. You have a tremendous rapport in your communication and will spend hours and hours just chatting about nothing. These people will really make you feel at ease.

Your connection with Leos born between the 15th and the 23rd of August will result in a beautiful love affair. You're passionate and sexual and both of you will bring that to the table, so to speak. This relationship will continue to be forever fresh and alive if you choose to make a go of it. There seems to also be a strong need for you to get outdoors and do things physically together. Seeing the world as a couple will stimulate and further cement your love for each other.

SAGITTARIUS + VIRGO
Fire + Earth = Lava

Virgo is not exactly your best match. Whereas you are a 'big picture' person, Virgo is primarily concerned with the details of life. Herein lies your first obstacle! And it could be a whopper of an obstacle, at that!

You're very different in your approaches to life. Sagittarians love to trust the process of life and invite the excitement of the unknown with open arms. Virgo needs to plan everything down to the letter. This will drive you crazy! These two patterns of character between you are so different, they're not easily reconciled.

Your views and those of Virgo are quite different and you'll both need to adjust considerably to make this relationship work. Try to be patient with Virgo when they become anxious about the details of life and their work. If you brush them off casually, this will not bode well and you will simply scare them away. You are intellectual in your own way, but Virgo needs to gain satisfaction by dealing with each and every detail. Accept that this is part of their internal design and don't hold it against them.

Virgo is the sign of the virgin, but this doesn't mean that sex is out of the question altogether, just that there's an innocence about how they prefer to deal with the intimate aspects of love. In this area you may also need to work harder to develop harmony in your romance. Strangely, you'll find Virgo inventive in the bedroom and your generous, loving gestures will draw Virgo out of themselves. For a while at least, your relationship could sizzle… for a while.

Virgo is very concerned with the concept of service, especially those born between the 3rd and the 12th of September. In this way, they will work for you, supporting your cause. They may not be as active as you are but are probably more intellectually orientated. They'll help you focus your energy and this can be a great practical asset to you, even if the relationship sexually and emotionally doesn't set the world alight.

You have a naturally magnetic attraction to Virgos born between the 24th of August and the

2nd of September, but this is primarily a professional connection. You may meet each other in a workplace scenario or through your profession and it could lead to a greater interest in each other. However, a romantic involvement may take considerable time to get off the ground.

Those Virgos born between the 13th and the 23rd of September irritate you, so it's best to play the waiting game before becoming too involved. You need to understand these individuals a little more before committing yourself to them. You are not at all compatible because you have so many divergent views. This bunch of Virgos will certainly be a challenge for you.

SAGITTARIUS + LIBRA
Fire + Air = Hot Air

Both of you regard each other as charming and, especially because Libra is ruled by Venus, you'll instantaneously feel love and attractiveness oozing out of them. With your Libran partner you will receive constant attention and demonstrativeness because Libra is one of the most social, loving and expressive signs of the zodiac.

Libra too is an air sign, which will fuel the fire of your soul. This is a great match because your elements are just so very compatible. You'll discover that this is a great two-way relationship, based upon communication and consideration. With you having fire as your Sagittarian element, and Libra being an air sign, we see that the flames of your Sagittarian fire will burn brightly in the company of your Libran counterpart. Your warmth will also uplift and generate a great deal of inspiration for your Libran partner.

This is a combination that can exhibit all the best traits of a relationship, including friendship, romance and good financial understanding. Librans make great friends to Sagittarius and support them in all of their endeavours. They can bring out the better qualities of your character.

Your social experiences together are quite fulfilling. but there is the tendency for both of you to overdo it. Remember the saying 'less is more' in your relationship.

With each person being footloose and fancy-free, the two of you will need to talk about balancing independence with commitment. You are both similar in this respect. Therefore the longevity of this relationship will rest upon how well you understand each other's needs and also, to a large extent, how much you are prepared to concede for each other. Both of you may in some ways be commitment phobic, at least initially.

Regarding sexuality, the two of you are very well suited and never stop trying to find ways to please each other. Just the fact that you're willing to consider the other person's needs inspires your partner, and the word 'passionate' could probably best describe your intimate connection.

Librans are generally a little fickle, but those born between the 24th of September and the 3rd of October seem utterly unstable, to your way of thinking. However, their love of independence does mirror your own approach to life, so in the case of a relationship with these people, it's a matter of 'what's good for the goose, is good for the gander'.

With Librans born between the 4th and the 13th of October, you'll discover a progressive way of doing things and existing in a relationship. These individuals are crazy but just so much fun, and you'll find their laughter quite infectious as well. You can expect the unexpected with them but you'll also be challenged to have to adjust yourself immensely from time to time.

You can expect a wonderful romance and even the opportunity of marriage with Librans born between the 14th and the 23rd of October. Gemini and Mercury have some influence over these interesting characters and, if other astrological factors are conducive, a long-term committed relationship or even marriage is quite likely. You have a strong sense of destiny with them and this relationship should be rewarding for both you.

SAGITTARIUS + SCORPIO

Fire + Water = Steam

Scorpio is the consummate investigator, researcher and interrogator. You're quite happy to encourage these extraordinary personality traits in your

Scorpio partner, as long as they don't overstep the bounds of good taste by prying into your business, or trying to control, dominate and possess you. Scorpio does have a tendency to come on a bit too strongly, which could scare you a little.

Scorpio is intense in their love, to say the least, whereas you, Sagittarius, enjoy the freedom and independence that comes naturally from being born under your star sign. In this relationship, personal liberty versus control will be the main topic of debate upon which its success or failure rests.

The big advantage with Sagittarius and Scorpio is the fact your ruling planets are very friendly and therefore this is always a good basis for a loving relationship. The co-ruler of Scorpio, Mars, and your own ruler, Jupiter, work together to produce big plans and far-sightedness, so this will endow your relationship with the same qualities. Together your dreams will manifest and are likely to give you immense success together.

There's a great crossover in your mental outlooks, which will result in both of you enjoying and sharing your ideas—political, psychological, religious and spiritual. Educational pursuits are mutually desirable so it's quite likely you will enrol in courses, go to lectures, and enjoy theatrical and cinema nights out together because you value your intellectual growth highly. You will also learn much from each other because the two of you are probably quite well read.

The Sagittarius and Scorpio match is a powerful sexual combination. You are excessive in most things and sex will be no exception. However, you must be careful this trait doesn't have a detrimental effect on the relationship in the long run by over-shadowing other positive aspects between you and your partner.

Scorpio has a tendency to hold onto grudges and sometimes they find it hard to let go of the past; but with you by their side, doing this could be much easier. Your busy social life and love of the great outdoors will help distract them from any negative emotions that can often get the better of some of them.

With Scorpios born between the 24th of October and the 2nd of November, you will strike up a great partnership. This will be a fiery and passionate relationship and it is one of the best matches with those born under the sign of Scorpio.

Going beyond the combination I've just mentioned, an even better relationship can be expected with Scorpios whose birth dates fall between the 3rd and the 12th of November. You'll find that Jupiter and Neptune have a considerable influence over these individuals, bringing out their creative, intuitive and spiritual nature. They are more than willing to help and support you in any way and they are selfless and compassionate people, being very universal in their views.

Love with a Scorpio born between the 13th and the 22nd of November is a mixture of happiness, misunderstanding and confusion. This is because the changeable Moon rules them and you may find it hard keeping up with the fluctuations of their temperament.

SAGITTARIUS + SAGITTARIUS
Fire + Fire = Explosion

You are clearly at an advantage if you choose to be with someone who sees eye to eye with you on most matters, being born under the same star sign. You could expect a wonderful relationship with another Sagittarian.

Because you are both fire signs, you are excited by what life has to offer. However, you do live hard and fast and you both agree that this relationship will need clear parameters, limits and guidelines to make it work on a practical level.

Your relationship with another Sagittarian might well explode and burn very brightly for a while, given that the two of you are fire signs and are highly combustible. But it may fizzle out just as quickly, too.

Commitment will be a key word and a difficult one for you both. You must vow either to stay with each other, or allow an open-style relationship. Honesty is, however, the great cornerstone of your relationship, so this is the perfect way for ensuring you've both pulled together and appreciate who you are. This connection will naturally allow both of you to tear down the walls that hinder you. This is a relationship based on integrity.

You can expect sexual fulfilment because you are magnanimous and caring towards each other, as well as offering loads of affection. Sagittarius has a forgiving nature so you're both likely to try to overlook the minor flaws in your personalities and appreciate the bigger picture.

There's a strong sense of competitiveness between you, but it normally appears in a friendly and fun way. Sagittarians born between the 23rd of November and the 1st of December will offer you this chance to play and compete and love. You're very compatible with these individuals because they have a great love of variety in relationships and enjoy social life as much as you do. This is a mutually supportive combination.

If you team up with a Sagittarian born between the 2nd and the 11th of December, they are strongly influenced by Mars and you will sense they have a formidable physical appetite. They are also particularly robust individuals, so keeping up with them may not be easy, except for the fact that you too are a Sagittarian. There's a great deal of comfort and sexual satisfaction to be discovered with these individuals. They participate in many outdoor activities and therefore this is a combination that is good for your physical health as well.

Sagittarians born during the period of the 12th to the 22nd of December have a touch of Leo in their personalities. They are very bright and attractive individuals, but they are also stubborn and love to control others. This could be a problem. If you're able to humble yourself, this relationship could actually become a long-term one.

SAGITTARIUS + CAPRICORN
Fire + Earth = Lava

You and Capricorn are so very different that commencing a relationship with them begs the question, why would you entertain this idea? You must never allow either of you to be pushed into a relationship, particularly if you come from cultures where there is an expectation you must stay together. I say this because of the fact that you're poles apart in your personalities. Having a sense of obligation forced upon you is no way to make a romantic association work.

Saturn, the solitary planet, rules Capricorn, and this makes them cool, detached, practical and conservative, to say the least. Jupiter, which rules your sign of Sagittarius, is open, warm, expansive and speculative. As you can see, the energies ruling both of you are diametrically opposed in every way. You are just so optimistic but Capricorn will somehow bring you down due to their seriousness.

You have a trusting nature and can't fathom why and how Capricorn is so suspicious of everything. They rarely trust anyone; unlike you, who seems to trust everyone. The best advice for both of you is to try to foster a happy balance between the two extremes, if possible.

Capricorn is quite possessive of not only their material belongings but of the ones they love. This jealous streak in their personality is something you find hard to deal with. You can't quite understand why they are so overly concerned with money, so cool in their affections, and just so traditional. Does any of this really stoke your fire? I think not.

I may seem to be painting a rather dull picture of Capricorn. But this is simply because they are slow to warm up. Once they do you'll find that, even though their sexual chemistry is not as hot as yours and not as compatible as you would like, they can, with time, make you feel comfortable and will be loving and loyal in their responses.

If you choose a relationship with a Capricorn born between the 23rd of December and the 1st of January, don't expect too much passion from them, at least not in the early stages. These characters are very down-to-earth and need heaps of persuasion to bring them around to your warm, loving and passionate ways.

You'll be surprised when I tell you that there are some emotional and sensual Capricorns, and those are likely to be born between the 2nd and the 10th of January. However, it will take you sometime to dig beneath the surface to see this in them, if you want to find it. Strangely, you are attracted to them and they are, in a similar fashion, drawn to you as well.

If you team up with a Capricorn born between the 11th and the 20th of January, you'll have an enjoyable time and will feel stimulated by their energies. They have a good sense of humour, but it is still rather dry and cynical. If you keep an open mind and exercise some patience, you might find that these Capricorn-born individuals can satisfy you, much to your surprise.

SAGITTARIUS + AQUARIUS
Fire + Air = Hot Air

It's highly unlikely you won't find an Aquarian-born individual appealing. The moment you meet them you'll realise that they are forward thinking, bright and original in every way.

Aquarius is an air sign and stimulates you on all levels. You feel as if you are learning something new each time you hang out with them. Like you, they enjoy freedom but can be rather unpredictable, so you need to be on your toes ready to head off in any direction at a moment's notice.

The Aquarian is an individualistic, self-willed and sometimes argumentative character. Their arguments can also frustrate you because often they are so aloof and detached in their manner that you get the feeling they're not arguing from any real emotional connection to their beliefs, but simply arguing for the sake of it. Sometimes Aquarians are irritable and also demanding, whereas you prefer a more laidback approach to life.

You're intrigued by the progressive attitude of Aquarius and the fact that they like to be constantly engaged with social and communal activities. Apart from the usual theatrical or club scene, Aquarius is genuinely interested in helping the world and doing something worthwhile. Because of your own leanings towards spirituality, these concepts appeal to you. You could find common ground in these areas.

Aquarius will, however, change your outlook on life because some of their ideas are so far-reaching they can open your eyes to the hidden, untried and untested. Being as adventurous as you are, you'll be thrilled by the idea of going where no one has gone before!

There's a great sexual rapport between Sagittarius and Aquarius because fire and air feed each other's needs. You'll both enjoy your moments of intimacy and this could turn out to be a rather long-lasting relationship.

If you want to get involved with an Aquarian born between the 21st and the 30th of January, get ready for some wonderful surprises. Firstly, you'll note they are particularly inflexible in their thinking, being as strongwilled as they are. You might find confrontations emerging regularly with them, so you need to think twice about a serious relationship if neither of you is flexible enough to give a little.

Those Aquarians born between the 31st of January and the 8th of February have a touch of Gemini influencing them. Due to this, marriage or a lifelong friendship is likely to result from your connection with them. You will both feel fulfilled in a relationship together.

Strong romantic indicators are present in a relationship with Aquarians born between the 9th and the 19th of February. Your love planet Venus has an influence on them, too, which means your soul will be soothed by being in their company. They will make you feel loved, cherished and honoured. This has all the hallmarks of an excellent long-term relationship, if not marriage.

SAGITTARIUS + PISCES

Fire + Water = Steam

So you are attracted to the dreamiest of the star signs—Pisces? They are the spiritual, psychic and selfless natives of the zodiac. Pisceans appeal to you probably because one of their ruling planets, Jupiter, also rules Sagittarius. You have a natural affinity with them.

Pisceans are perceptive, but themselves are often hard to figure out. You like someone who has self-initiative, is self-directed and ambitious. Pisces doesn't always fit the bill on these counts.

They are, however, loving, caring and sexually very giving. You will click sexually with your Piscean lover and find their affection and loving ways addictive. As long as they don't hold back, you'll probably hang in there with your Piscean lover and enjoy what this relationship has to offer.

The domestic side of Pisces and their nurturing ways make them excellent family people. They feel creative as nurturers and carers and you'll never be in need if you choose to spend the rest of your life with them. Trying to get them to think practically or in the way that the average person thinks is another matter, but you'll always be loved and supported by them in their own way.

The sign of Sagittarius is known for its philosophical curiosity, but Pisces is practical in the application and expression of its philosophical ideals. This is where Pisces can act as an important karmic teacher for Sagittarius in a relationship, not just on a romantic level but on the level of friendship, too.

Those Pisceans born between the 20th and the 28th or 29th of February have many similar interests to you and are quite intuitive and spiritual in their aspirations. You'll never be able to hide anything from them, so don't try it. Their hunches are usually correct.

Take your time if you want to get into a relationship with a Piscean born between the 1st and the 10th of March. They're extremely sensitive, emotional and overreact to trifles. Take care how you approach them because they're particularly finicky about many aspects of life, not the least of which is money. If you're a spendthrift, this could also be a problem with them.

If you choose a relationship with a Piscean born between the 11th and the 20th of March, this will be a positive experience. The planets Mars, Pluto and Jupiter have a strong influence over their personalities. There's something clandestine or secretive about this relationship, so you should expect a different type of love if you're serious about going all the way with them.

SAGITTARIUS

2010:
The Year Ahead

*To solve a problem or to reach a goal, you… don't
need to know all the answers in advance. But you must
have a clear idea of the problem or the goal you want
to reach.*

—W. Clement Stone

Romance and friendship

For most Sagittarians, 2010 is likely to be particularly
fortunate for your interpersonal life, especially in
the first month of the year, with Jupiter favourably
influencing your zone of marriage, partnerships and
karmic relationships. You have the perfect opportunity to seek out and connect with people who
understand you and who will be prepared to satisfy
your emotional, mental, spiritual and physical needs.
Your lucky planet Mars highlights this fact as well
early in the year, as it moves higher in the heavens,
blessing you with energy, drive and good fortune in
all of your meetings.

You are concerned about finding your ideal
partner this year. Although you may come across
many people who would ordinarily be to your
liking, your standards will be much higher than they
usually are and you won't get involved with all of
them.

Mars is strongly connected with such things
as your love affairs and also sexual activity. Being
in your zone of ethics for much of the year, it shows
you will primarily be interested in working through
some of your past issues that previously have held
you back from finding meaning in your life.

This will be more pronounced if you are in a committed relationship, or married, and are finding your interests with your partner diverging. It will be necessary for you throughout January, at the outset of the year, to discuss any differences that are outstanding so you can move forward with the special person you love.

You will be intense in your feelings and not at all interested in light or casual affairs or one-night stands, although Sagittarius does have a reputation for being rather free spirited. That will all change in 2010. This year will be remembered as the one when you turned the corner to attract what you feel you deserve romantically.

Your passions are highlighted due to the influence on you of Mars and Venus, which may spur you to travel, even considerable distances, to be with those whom you feel are compatible with you. Considerable charm will be at your fingertips and you will be attractive, to say the least.

Much of your focus will be on peace of mind and finding inner happiness during 2010. During March and April you will be clear in your understanding of the fact that the success of your relationships is strongly tied in with creating as much domestic bliss as you can. With Mercury, Jupiter, the Sun, Venus and Uranus all populating your zone of family, domestic activities and inner happiness, you will be forced, in spite of yourself, to deal with these issues throughout this part of the year.

The full Moon in March will also highlight much

of your inner feelings and you will discover a whole new approach to handling your domestic circumstances, relatives and, in particular, your mother and older women in your life.

When the Sun transits your zone of love affairs throughout April, great opportunities to socialise can be expected. Of course, there are some tensions as well, due not only to your desire to continue to explore all of the novel and unexpected facets of life, but also by the need to secure your future and keep your personal life on a steadier path. These tensions will be caused by Saturn and Uranus, two very opposing forces in the zodiac. Nevertheless, you'll be thrilled by some of the experiences that life throws your way and, needless to say, the people who cross your path at this time will make a huge impact on you.

Saturn has an important role to play in your friendships throughout 2010, and this may not be one of the easier effects to diffuse. You are always very optimistic in the way you view life and see everything as an opportunity rather than a problem. Unfortunately, not everyone views life in the same way that you do and, in fact, during May and June, you may have to deal with those who are negative or even downright sarcastic and insulting about your ways of doing things. Because of this you may realise in a flash that not everyone is meant to be with you forever.

Be careful of who you invite into your life around June, because Venus and Pluto indicate incredibly obsessive or intense moods and relationships around you. You'd hate to invite a stalker into your life, which is what may happen here if you are less than willing to scrutinise others' characters. Look more carefully at what other people's intentions might be.

Sexual matters, deep-seated fears or other hidden issues in your relationships could start to resurface around July. The intensity of Pluto continues and has an impact on Mercury and the Sun. If you don't want to hear the answers to some of your questions, it's best not to go snooping or prying. You may be suspicious of your partner and will be in two minds as to whether or not to get to the bottom of the situation, or simply let things slide. It's likely that you'll prefer to honour the truth, even if what you hear causes you some grief, albeit temporarily.

In July and August, seeking out educational programs that can bring you more in touch with yourself is a good idea. With Venus, Mars and Saturn transiting the upper part of your horoscope, and with Neptune acting as an opposing force to these three planets, you'll want to make heads or tails of your life and know how this will impact on your relationships.

Bringing structure into your life will become more and more important from this time on and, sometimes, it's not at all embarrassing to admit you just don't know where to start. This is where mentors or those older and more experienced can bring you to the state of self-understanding. Someone at this time may act as a catalyst to bring you some greater self-awareness that will help you transition to the next phase of your life.

Although much of your tension begins to release after September, you'll still be dealing with some issues, especially those of friendships, during September. Someone from your past whom you thought you may have dealt with and had gotten rid of may re-enter the picture to cause you further anxiety. You may not know how to say 'no', but this is the mantra I should drum into your head at this time: say 'no'. If you understand full well that history can and does repeat itself, by using this simple two-letter word, you may be able to sidestep the usual catastrophes that befall others who don't learn from their past mistakes.

At the same time, you will note that things are not going all that well between people around you, and you may have to act as a mediator to bring peace to the group. Remaining passively impartial under these circumstances could be a major challenge for you, but unless you want to lose one or more friends, this is precisely what you will have to do. The diplomat within you will need to shine.

Your passion is still strong in October but away from public view. In other words, it may be a great time to get away with the one you love to a quiet, romantic place where no one can see or hear you. Recharge your batteries and reconnect with the one you love in a mode of silence. This is a spiritual break for you, but one that can also further cement your love for your other half.

In October and November you may carefully need to analyse and deal with the difficulties associated with a sibling or someone whom you consider a brother or sister. Problems may weigh heavily on them and your generous nature will have no option but to step in and help them. Circumstances out of their control will be of particular concern to you. This is your chance to act as a mentor and guide for them during their turbulent times.

Mercury, the planet ruling your marital affairs, will be in difficulty during late November and throughout December. This is because of its proximity to Mars, the warring and argumentative force of nature. Try not to be too belligerent or overbearing in your opinions and, even if you think others are acting this way, listen patiently without dismissing them. Certainly, this will be a phase of the year in which your nerves will be severely tested. But if you're able to forebear the difficult personalities of those you love and associate with, you'll come out of this last portion of 2010 a much better, stronger and insightful human being.

Work and money

Venus, Pluto, the Sun and Mercury all have a say in your finances as 2010 kicks off. You are intense, desirous of earning money and having a greater, wealthier lifestyle throughout this period. But unfortunately greater economic trends will create challenges for you and patience will be necessary to achieve your goals. Overcoming financial greed, excess and wastefulness are your key motivations throughout January, February and March. Bring these three internal forces under strict control so you can acquire more and do it in an efficient and timely manner.

One advantage you have in January is the occupation of Jupiter, your ruling planet, in your third zone of communications and contracts. Tie up loose ends early in the year, state your case, and don't compromise on any contractual fine print if you are negotiating business matters. You will come out a winner.

Purchasing property will be beneficial for you, but don't expect a quick fix. When Jupiter and Uranus move into close proximity after April, in May, something sudden and exciting can occur. If some of you have felt thwarted in your attempts to sell property, a willing buyer may appear out of nowhere. May is also a great time for starting partnerships, commencing a new business or generally dealing with the public. Venus is well placed to bring you popularity and additional income throughout this period of the year.

With less pressure from Saturn due to its exit from your zone of business profit, April, May and June should be much more favourable months for increasing your income, asking for that pay rise, or taking a punt on a new position and going for that job interview. Saturn retrogrades back into your zone of career and tells us that there's no gain without a little pain. You can expect good results, but be prepared for the additional pressure of more responsibility, even though you may be seeing a fatter pay cheque each month.

You can feel quite overwhelmed in July and August by work matters. Put this down to Mars and Saturn being in the uppermost part of your horoscope. Working long hours may take its toll on you, so don't forget to be gentle on yourself and pace yourself at the same time. Get exercise and plenty of rest because you're going to need it. However, Mercury and Venus do bring good opportunities and also hint at the fact that you have some great support, even though you may have overlooked it.

Seek out friendships among those in your peer group or even employers who are sympathetic to your difficult position and excessive workloads. Surprisingly, someone may come forward to help and this will be of considerable relief to you.

Your passion for work and success is reignited in September with Venus and Mars providing you ample fuel to move forward. The Moon also shows us that you are somewhat emotional in your approach to the public, so try to use your head rather than your heart when conducting any business. This may even relate to shopping at your local mall, where something catches your eye and you decide then and there that you want it. If you're convinced that the new television set or lounge suite is not going to be available tomorrow or the day after, remind yourself there's no rush and that it's best to shop about and also get the approval of your partner!

Don't let people talk you into parting with money until you've done your homework. In October, Venus and Mars in your zone of expenses show that you're rather wasteful, if not negligent, in the way you are conducting yourself. Get some advice on how better to manage your money, especially if you start to see the bills piling up. The Sun and Saturn in your zone of profitability show a curtailing of your income at this time as well. You may have been promised extra bonuses only to find that the economy has slowed a little and these may be postponed. Moderation will be your primary key word.

In November and December you are quite dynamic with Mars entering your Sun sign. You have a desire to show what you can do and most likely you'll be able to. But remember, not everyone is going to be able to keep up with you. Mars makes you rash, impulsive and also a little overbearing. If you want the support of your co-workers, try to be lenient, especially if you're in command. To gain respect you have to give respect.

It's at this time of the year when you realise that pressing deadlines may be further intensified by the fact that Christmas and the excessive requests of family members make you time-poor as well. Planning effectively will be critical throughout the final two months of 2010. If you can do that, you'll manage both your personal and business affairs wisely and enjoy what Christmas 2010 has to offer. All in all, this year should turn out to be quite favourable and fulfilling, personally and financially.

Karma, luck and meditation

Developing and expressing your highest and best self requires the elimination of old, ingrained habits. The year 2010 is an important one for you to realise that recognising your bad behaviour patterns and reversing them are the keys to your success.

In January, Venus and Pluto, coupled with the Sun and Mercury, set the trend for a heightened desire for acquiring material possessions. It's important to learn economy by cutting back on waste and exercising moderation in all things, not just your finances. By redirecting these primal forces of nature, you can develop your creative instincts and produce some of the finest work possible in the coming twelve months. This will then afford you inner satisfaction as well as financial rewards.

Mars, one of your karmic planets, transits your ninth zone of philosophy, foreign culture and morality this year. Note carefully that this planet tenants this area of your horoscope for six months. I can't stress enough how important Mars will be to your development in 2010, particularly with respect to your psychic abilities, insights into others, and spiritual wisdom. This is a year where understanding life and your place in it will have long-term ramifications.

You'll be tested in August and September, reflecting the old saying that, 'what doesn't kill you only makes you stronger'. Although your work and family lives and the people associated with these areas will be demanding and test your inner resolve and the limits of your patience, by handling it all, you will emerge from the other end stronger and wiser for doing so.

Meditation, yoga practices and other spiritual activities will be attractive to you in October and November, with your twelfth zone of secrets and meditative issues taking the spotlight. By engaging yourself in inward study and self-reflection, you'll balance the other exciting and successful material aspects of life in 2010.

SAGITTARIUS

2010:
Month By Month
Predictions

*Experience is that marvellous thing that enables you to
recognise a mistake when you make it again.*

—F.P. Jones

Highlights of the month

You're confronted with important practical decisions this month due to a lunar eclipse on the 1st.
Not only your own personal income but that of your
partner and business associates too, will be impli-
cated in these powerful celestial energies.

Between the 5th and the 12th, you'll have very
little time to do much else than contemplate your
financial strategies and what you need to do to get
back on track, economically speaking.

An excellent retrograde movement of Saturn in
your profit sector is a good omen and shows that,
from the 14th onwards, there could be some relief
in terms of these financial pressures we're talking
about.

Great dynamic energy can be expected from the 15th, because Mars favourably influences your Sun sign at this time. Being high up in your chart, your sense of adventure is very powerfully activated and will draw you into a whole lot of new investigations. New friendships, journeys and seeking out new places of employment are some of the likely outcomes of this transit for you.

Contractual arrangements, notifications or courses of action that have been held in abeyance move forward between the 16th and the 20th. Whereas early in the month you'll be unable to firmly decide on a course of action, now you'll be much more decisive, and have the support of everyone involved due to this forward motion of Mercury and a very powerful solar eclipse in your finances sector.

Between the 22nd and the 25th, Venus and the Sun favourably influence Saturn, indicating that you will acquire a better position, higher self-esteem among friends and a likely pay rise, if that's on the cards for you. In any case, you'll be more diligent and clear upon your purpose and should be paid for your good work.

You need to direct your energies carefully between the 26th and the 28th, when Venus and Mars cause you to act irrationally in love. Your sense of adventure may get the better of you, and being impulsive is not out of the question. Try to see the practical side of a situation, especially if your emotions are involved. At this time you're likely to believe there is more to someone than there actually is.

You could be accident prone around the 30th, which can be put down to the tough transit of the Sun and Mars. Don't be in a rush to get to your destination and, in personal relationships, listen to the other person's viewpoint before hitting them over the head with a sledgehammer. There may be greater sense in what they're saying than you are at first willing to acknowledge.

Neptune opposes your career sector during this phase of your life, so it's likely there is some confusion over what you should be doing. Again, bring clarity and intellect into the picture, and don't rely wholly and solely on your emotions to make your decisions.

Romance and friendship

The lunar eclipse in your zone of sexuality on the 1st is a powerful influence, indicating more intimacy and the need to understand your feelings as well as the feelings of those you love.

Between the 2nd and the 5th, sex and your life values will tie together and require much discussion with your spouse or partner. You mustn't use money or other material values as a substitute for true intimacy. You'll become very clear on this point.

With the Sun and Venus conjoining between the 10th and 12th your popularity will become much stronger. However, you might find that by the 14th you've had enough of the late nights and could feel the pressure. Take time out, especially around the solar eclipse of the 15th, when you can totally recharge your batteries.

With Saturn moving retrograde around this time you might need to have some serious discussions with a close friend between the 16th and 17th. Don't let your emotions get the better of you and stick to the point at hand. Furthermore, there's no need to rehash the past because this could inflame the situation.

Family affairs are pleasant and bring you gifts and accolades between the 18th and 20th. Visitors such as relatives or distant friends coming to stay with you need extra attention, but it will be worth it.

From the 25th to the 30th your marital or personal affairs are not exactly going to plan. Keep a level-head and don't react too strongly to words from others. Maintain the peace.

Work and money

You'll probably feel disinclined to worry about your work or finances, but around the 4th or 5th your mind will kick into gear and start to focus very strongly on financial matters.

On the 7th, seriously consider the sources of your income and whether or not everything is above board. Make sure you're writing receipts for the same amounts given to you from others so you can keep your records squeaky clean.

Expenses are high between the 10th and 12th, but at this time an increase in income should be expected.

Around the 13th you are obsessive about some financial matter or situation in which you feel you haven't been fairly treated.

Major changes will take place after the 15th, when the solar eclipse brings to light many hidden aspects to your finances, professional activities and workplace connections.

New contracts should commence around the 16th, or at least discussions on how to give you a better deal.

Investment property and other financial matters, including expenses related to your home, are in the front of your mind from the 19th through until the 25th.

Destiny dates

Positive: 14, 15, 16, 17, 18, 19, 20, 22, 23, 24, 25
Negative: 26, 27, 28, 30
Mixed: 1, 5, 12

Highlights of the month

There are times in your life when the way you think and feel is completely out of sync with those around you. In February, try to think like others, even if at heart you know your way is better. Between the 3rd and the 8th, you'll realise that what you want may be just so different from what others desire.

For example, the way you want to dress and express yourself in terms of fashion may be out of step with the prevailing codes, especially in a professional environment. You might have no choice but to do what others do until a more appropriate time for individual expression is presented to you.

Jupiter is favourable for you now and, as it moves through your zone of family, inner peace and domestic affairs, it's likely you'll expand your awareness of these things, and also put more energy into making this part of your life much happier and more secure.

Venus also supports this fact, especially after

the 11th, when it too comes to join Jupiter in your zone of domestic affairs. If you've had any troubles with family members, neighbours or other figures from your past history, this is the time when good feelings abound and you can bury the hatchet and take these relationships to a whole new level.

You're also prompted to spend big, especially if you haven't been satisfied with any aspect of your living space. You have the opportunity to call in a builder or an architect to modify your domestic arenas, especially if you feel cramped or your house's colour scheme is not quite to your liking. It's the perfect time to bring things into harmony and, even if it costs you a bit of money, you'll be more than happy to make this investment.

From the 13th till the 19th there are some disturbing effects caused by Mercury and Mars. In your most personal relationships and friendships, be careful that your opinions don't rub up people the wrong way. It could be that you realise just how different your philosophies are to those with whom you normally spend time.

It's all about respecting the other person's viewpoint, even if they don't happen to respect yours. You could be tested. However, you have the broadmindedness to allow them to believe what they want and to assert yourself quietly, even without words if necessary.

Spiritual and meditative energies are strong after the 25th, when Venus and the Sun produce deeper intuition, stronger dreams and foresight. Trust your instincts at this time because they'll be right on the money. If you don't feel comfortable about something or someone, don't go against that still, small, inner voice. It will now serve you well.

Romance and friendship

You are excitable this month but Venus and Neptune also make you confused in love. On the one hand you are passionate, impulsive and idealistic about who you want to be with, but also reluctant to give of yourself on the 3rd. Around the 7th your energies come to the fore and blast you with a dose of self-confidence again.

If you meet someone around the 3rd who appears to be your ideal soulmate, you may find it difficult to focus on little else up until the 12th. You'll be obsessive and unable to contemplate other things. Try your best to put it all in perspective before giving away your power to someone else.

The 14th, Valentine's Day, is a communicative day with much activity and discussion between you, friends and others whom you may meet in a social setting. Stimulating ideas inspire you to do something alternative and associate with those who think differently to you.

A great flow of energy is indicated by the Moon in Jupiter between the 15th and 16th. You feel more loving towards your family members, even those who previously have been difficult and hard to understand.

The period of the 17th until the 22nd is excellent for cementing your relationships and spending quality time with the one you love.

You could discover something about yourself or your loved one on the 24th. Use this to your advantage, even if at first the idea seems quirky. It could make your life just that little bit more interesting. Try not to be too harsh a judge of others.

Long-distance romance is on the cards between the 26th and 28th. Signing up with an online dating site could be something you might like to consider, even if in the past you have shunned this as a means of making contact with a potential lover.

Work and money

Someone could be instrumental in helping you in your work, probably a woman who is well connected, especially between the 1st and 4th. She may appear on the heels of someone else who previously had promised you an introduction, only to let you down.

Between the 5th and the 9th, spend some time alone away from others. You'll get much more done, especially if you are working with someone who is irritating, annoying and demands more of your time and attention than you care to give them.

You could be confused about some contractual issues around the 14th. If you don't understand the topic at hand, don't let your ego get in the way of asking for assistance and getting further explanation and clarity.

You can make a big impact on the general public after the 22nd. You have your finger on the pulse and your charm will work wonders. For salespeople and other executives dealing with the population at large, this is an excellent time to make headway in your career.

Take some precautions on the 26th, especially if you're feeling aggressive. Maybe it is best to postpone a few appointments until you are feeling better.

Destiny dates

Positive: 1, 2, 20, 21, 22, 23, 24, 25, 26, 27, 28

Negative: 13

Mixed: 3, 4, 5, 6, 7, 8, 9, 10, 11, 12, 14, 15, 16, 17, 18, 19

Highlights of the month

This year you want to create a better family environment. However, during March there might be just a little too much energy focused here, even for your liking. The spotlight is most definitely on this area of your life, with Mercury, Jupiter, the Sun, Venus and Uranus all magnifying their energies on this one aspect. Expansion, expenditure and inter-relationships may be overwhelming. It's imperative for you to pace yourself, particularly when Mercury enters the picture on the 2nd.

Around the 7th, when Venus triggers your romantic instincts (and suddenly, at that) you may have divided loyalties. On the one hand you will want to fulfil the assurances you've given to commitments at home, but on the other will want to explore some newfound relationship. The wild and wonderful will need to be balanced with the conservative demands of your clan.

Passion is further aroused around the 8th with

Venus in favourable aspect to Mars at this time. You are driven to express your passion, irrespective of what anyone else seems to think. This is a highly creative period as well, and it could well be that a person you meet at this time may themselves be creative and can trigger your own expression. It's a perfect time to join forces with someone of like mind and to pursue some noble activity together while developing the intimate aspects of a relationship.

As your passions strongly emerge there is also another side to the equation and this is associated with some friendship. The cooling effect of Venus and Saturn between the 9th and the 15th could see you pulling away from someone in your group of friends. This may not be anything to be alarmed about, but could simply be just a passing phase, or part of their own cycle in which they need to spend time alone.

It's best to give them the space they need rather than imagining too much is wrong. This phase will pass soon enough for them and, of course, it gives you the opportunity to pursue other affairs and friendships, as we've just mentioned above.

Around the 14th, you're more directed in your professional domains. Physically, too, your life forces could be much stronger. Get into some wholesome physical activities and utilise this energy to improve your health and wellbeing generally.

If you happen to be a parent, from the 18th you're likely to reconnect in a very satisfying way with children. Mercury adds a touch of zest and humour to the relationship and you'll be surprised at just how communicative youngsters are with you during this phase of the year. Incidentally, you may learn something from them as well, so don't close the door to what is offered just because someone happens to be considerably younger than you are. They may have a different spin on a situation and it will help you.

After the 22nd, spend some time listening to the problems of a friend, because you may be able to help them through their dilemma. This won't require any special counselling skills because you will just 'know' what to say at the right time.

Romance and friendship

You'll realise after the 2nd that you can't maintain an emotionally messy backyard and expect to have success in love. You'll be curious about how to increase your inner peace and harmony so as to attract someone of like mind. This will be even more important around the 4th when you suddenly attract someone who is completely unexpected and different from the usual type of person you meet.

Venus enters your fifth zone of love affairs around the 7th and heralds the commencement of a new and positive phase in your romantic affairs. Expect to meet many new people but also to feel an upswing in your level of creativity. Your general aura will be bright and so it is hardly surprising that this will be an attractive and fun period for you.

Your values will be changing this month, as is evidenced by the forward motion of Mars around the 11th. This occurs in your zone of ethics, philosophical and religious views and some of your morals may now be challenged.

On the 13th trust your instincts and your spiritual insights to give you the answers you are seeking, especially if you are confronted by a dilemma as to which way to go in some new friendship.

The health of a younger person causes you some concerns between the 18th and 22nd. Your own health, too, may be a problem, so take some time and the appropriate measures to make sure your vitality is at its optimum. Too many late nights, partying and an excessive lifestyle is the source.

Between the 27th and 31st you could be so drained by work and other personal concerns that you find it hard to hand out the energy your partner wants from you. If necessary, explain to them that you need some time out to rethink your position.

Work and money

Between the 2nd and the 4th there's a connection between your earning capacity and your home life. Clear out the basement, the attic or that spare room and turn it into an area where you can create some value for yourself. This is the perfect time to consider an independent financial lifestyle through working at something you love.

After the 7th speculation is rife and you can invest in something that pays off. Metals, minerals and other products of the Earth are favoured in this respect.

Debts, delays in payments and lost receipts or indeed lost valuables may be issues for you between the 19th and the 23rd. Keep a close eye on your valuables and don't leave your bag lying around where it is easy for it to be mislaid or even stolen.

Destiny dates

Positive: 3, 4, 7, 8, 18
Negative: 19, 20, 23, 27, 28, 29, 30
Mixed: 2, 9, 10, 11, 12, 13, 14, 15, 22

Highlights of the month

Don't go spending too much time worrying about what is being said about you, or who happens to be your enemy. Between the 1st and the 4th you may hear rumours or gossip about yourself that can be rather disturbing. If this occurs in your workplace, it is far better for you to put your head down and focus on your work than try to investigate the source of these rumours.

Usually, if you think about it, such forms of gossip reflect some sort of envy, which you should take as a subtle form of flattery. Someone doesn't like you because you're probably doing well or are very efficient in the line of work you've chosen. Don't pay too much attention to it.

Jupiter creating a favourable aspect with the Sun is excellent for a sense of wellbeing this month, but may also cause you to spend heavily. Don't be impulsive, even if what you see is what you desire. Look around and shop wisely.

On the 5th and 6th, delays in communications are likely. Messages, e-mails, or important documents relating to your own health or the health of someone in your family may need to be chased up and could be lost or overlooked. Work on improving your filing system to avoid these issues in future.

Venus and Pluto create a somewhat obsessive state of mind in the first week of the month, and you must learn to let go, especially if you desire something that you can't have. By the 7th, your mind will be able to penetrate these layers of confusion and obsession, much to your advantage.

The flip side of this is that someone may be obsessing over you or something you have done! Convincing them to back off and let you do things in your own way could be a challenge and requires a great deal of diplomacy on your part.

When Saturn re-enters your zone of career around the 8th, you can expect much more responsibility to be thrown your way. It might happen intentionally, because by their nature, promotions usually incur an increased amount of responsibility, don't they? But if this is unintentional and something you haven't chosen, you could begrudge having to handle an extra dose of work for a while. There may be no way out of this, so the only advice I can give you is to grin and bear it. If you're able to delegate some of these further duties, that would be all the better for you.

Health issues may still be looming between the 15th and the 18th. An excessive lifestyle is bad for you, so try to moderate your diet, look into the way you combine the foods you do eat and, naturally, try to get more sleep, especially if the above mentioned workload is getting too much.

You'll need to discharge some additional debts around the 20th and could be in for a surprise if you haven't balanced your books too well. Try to set up a budget; look a little ahead to see what's coming rather than living hand to mouth. If you have credit cards, it may be the ideal time to pay them out or at least transfer them to another bank where a reduced interest rate is on offer.

Venus brings some social delights between the 25th and the 29th and is just what the doctor ordered. Enjoy yourself and let your hair down, at least for these few days.

Romance and friendship

In the first week of the month, especially between the 2nd and 4th, you need to pay close attention to the quality of service and support you have been giving the one you love. If you've been complaining about not receiving the love and backup you so desire, could it be that this reflects your poor input into the relationship?

The health of a lover may come into question between the 9th and the 14th, so you need to sacrifice a bit of your time to prove that you do love them.

The new Moon in your fifth zone of love affairs

is significant in that it can herald the start of a new relationship, new beginnings and emotional excitement. You could expect this to occur some time around the 15th or 16th.

By the 17th, when the Moon enters your zone of marriage, you might find yourself hitched to someone you truly believe is a worthwhile partner. If married or otherwise committed, this could be the start of a new phase in which you choose to re-ignite the flames of love and pursue a similar direction together.

The Sun moving through your zone of entertainment and hobbies, as well as sporting activities, after the 21st, is a lovely energy that stimulates you to express yourself, so take up a new interest and create some time for yourself. It's important to develop your self-esteem through appreciating your own value. This in turn will attract respectful people into your life.

On or about the 23rd you might hear news about an important celebrity or guest speaker visiting your town or locality and you have the opportunity to make a social night out of it. Take the initiative: ring your friends to get together for a wonderful evening that will also expand your mental horizons.

The period of the 25th to the 29th is excellent for combining learning with social engagements and a party-like atmosphere.

Work and money

After the 1st you'll want to spruce up your working environment. If you find yourself in drab surroundings, it is not exactly going to inspire your best work, is it? Why not give your area a colour makeover, add some plants and stimulate your mind through doing an interior design job on your office or workspace. It will work wonders.

You could find yourself disappointed around the 5th when a promise of extra money or a loan may fall through. You should have several avenues for finances lined up in case one doesn't work to your advantage.

By the 7th you could be finding yourself obsessing over monetary matters and you need to examine the real motivation for your dissatisfaction. Remember: the best things in life aren't things.

After the 8th Saturn moves to your tenth zone of professional activity and indicates the acquisition of a new position, or certainly at least more responsibility. These issues intensify up to and including the 26th, but only then will you be in the position to handle matters with dignity.

Destiny dates

Positive: 7, 21, 23, 25, 26, 27, 28, 29
Negative: 2, 3, 4, 5, 6, 9, 10, 11, 12, 13, 14, 20
Mixed: 1, 8, 15, 16, 17, 18

Highlights of the month

Much of your work this month will be intellectual and that goes for your relationships as well. From the 4th till the 8th, delving deeply into problems and finding unique solutions for them will not only fascinate you but may also take up considerable time.

You are keen to reorganise your working life, get things tidy and remove the backlog that may be bothering you during this first week of the month. Financial matters may also need careful attention, but you mustn't get angry at those who serve you. Accountants, lawyers and other practitioners who handle your accounts such as banking staff may be slow and sloppy in their work.

You'll be demanding a more meticulous service than you are receiving and could lose your cool under the circumstances. Between the 9th and the 15th, you need to act in a controlled way if you are to get the service you are after.

Dealing with older and more established people and institutions will be beneficial throughout May. Around the 19th, a favourable aspect between the Sun and Saturn augurs well for your professional activities. If you have progressive ideas, you must package them in a way that is going to be palatable to the more conventional members of your group.

This is not a time to scare people with your outlandish ideas. You can, however, make some headway by incorporating the old with the new. This way, people will be more likely to take on board the ideas you have. Of course, if you're in the driver's seat, you have a better opportunity of calling the shots and should take a gamble knowing that the idea is practical, has merit, and will ultimately give you good returns.

Partnerships are likely to be in the spotlight from the 20th. Shared resources, loans and other borrowings may be a feature of the negotiations. When the Sun comes to the zone of partnerships on the 21st, you can expect some good feedback and support, not only from your business partners but from your romantic partners as well. Your spouse or long-term friend will make you feel good and this is a time to connect strongly with them. Put aside other matters, at least up until the 23rd, so that you can enjoy the love you're meant to share as a couple.

From the 24th to the 28th, your desire to take a punt may pay off. Sudden and unexpected gains are likely at this time due to the influence of Uranus on your gambling and financial tendencies. Relationships are also likely to be just as exciting and perhaps you should take a punt on this as well.

Romance and friendship

You're particularly emotional about relationships this month and around the 2nd may find yourself thwarted in your attempts to express just how much you love someone else. They may be cool and disinterested, which could leave you feeling high and dry.

I suggest you can try to distract yourself mentally between the 5th and 9th, when the Moon and Mars enter into a strong aspect to each other. Your temper will be stimulated, so you need to be careful about how you ask for what you want. You could come across as demanding, belligerent or even egotistical. Be nice if you want people to give you what you need!

Expect some exciting times between the 10th and 15th. Uranus has a powerful effect on your nerves and you'll want to break free of the constraints of your lifestyle. Don't be carried away by the mood of the moment, too much alcohol, or promises of bigger and better things.

Nevertheless, this will be a creatively exciting period because it gives you the opportunity to do something out of the ordinary.

Sometime around the 21st you'll find yourself in two minds over your relationship. For singles this can be an interesting period inasmuch as a couple of people could be showing an interest in you. Making a choice between them could be difficult, although it is rather flattering, wouldn't you agree?

Someone born under the signs of Mercury, such as a Virgo or Gemini, may have a stronger than usual influence on your life.

Between the 29th and 31st someone could have some wonderful news relating to an engagement or wedding. You may be part of the celebration at this time and it may even extend to the birth of a new child within the family circle.

Work and money

It will be awfully difficult not to be distracted by your personal life this month and this is, to a large extent, due to the placement of Saturn in your zone of career.

Between the 3rd and 12th, you will feel weighed down by the excessive demands of an employer, or there may be some change in your workplace that requires some rather drastic adjustments.

Professional matters are improved between the 16th and 20th, with Venus offering you assistance by way of charm, popularity and additional bonuses or financial offers. If you are an independently orientated business person you may partner up with someone during this period to create a new business venture that is likely to be popular with the public.

The effect of receiving extra cash or a surplus of

money around the 23rd is short-lived. By the 27th to the 29th, you may have spent it all.

Destiny dates

Positive: 12, 13, 14, 15, 17, 18, 19, 20, 24, 25, 26, 30, 31

Negative: 2

Mixed: 3, 4, 5, 6, 7, 8, 9, 10, 11, 21, 23, 27, 28, 29

Highlights of the month

Between the 1st and the 5th, you'll be inclined to delve into the unknown. The tried and tested will not appeal to you all that much, but be careful because the unknown means you might not have the qualifications or the ability to handle what you discover. Don't let boredom be the motivating factor for your actions.

Venus is lucky for you between the 6th and the 9th, bringing you new friendships. You'll feel in tune with most of the people you meet, which may be surprising given that many of them might be complete strangers. Your karmic connections are strong.

Jupiter brings you a streak of luck in love and your financial life between the 10th and the 12th. You'll be confident in yourself, even if you find it hard to believe that others find you so wonderful. You must believe that what they're saying is true. Remove any self-doubts.

Venus moves through your ninth zone of travels and education. After the 14th, you can move full-steam ahead in your studies. Even if you're an older Sagittarian, it's never too late to learn, so get out those books and fulfil those dreams to become better than what you've been in the past.

Between the 16th and the 20th, journeys bring you lucky encounters, so you mustn't refuse an offer to travel or explore a new location. You've fallen into the trap of feeling comfortable in your habitual social environment. This is the time to venture out of your safety zone.

The 21st to the 23rd brings strange events your way, but these are positive. You'll need to go with the flow and not resist situations that you've not experienced before.

Between the 25th and the 27th, your imagination soars and you discover some new or latent talent that you never dreamed you could have. You must develop this and let it take you where it will.

A lunar eclipse occurs on the 26th and brings your finances into full view. It's the start of a new cycle, so don't be afraid to look at the situation fairly and squarely, even if what you see is not altogether to your liking. You have to acknowledge a problem exists before you can fix it.

After the 28th, the Sun and Mercury open your eyes to some new financial opportunities. Don't let fear deter you from exploring these new avenues, even if you feel you don't have the expertise to make them happen. Where there's a will, there's a way.

Romance and friendship

It's great to be appreciated and between the 1st and 5th you'll feel that this is the case, especially in respect of your career objectives. Your partner or best friend will want to outwardly show gestures of appreciation and may even offer to help share the load at this time.

After the 7th it's not a good idea to push yourself too much. Pat yourself on the back and buy yourself a gift. It is important to appreciate yourself, just as it is for others to appreciate you.

There could be a few tensions in the air between the 8th and 10th when someone in your vicinity tries to interfere with what you think is the correct course of action. This is not necessarily a major drama but could cause a bit of strain over a few days.

Emotional mind games resurface around the 13th, including selfishness, jealousy and perhaps some form of emotional blackmail, too. If your relationships are unsettled, it is time to bring such issues to the surface and get them out of the way, once and for all. This is essential for your development as a couple or marital partners.

You are advised to listen on the 18th when a conversation can get rather intense and heavy. If you are intellectually lazy at some luncheon or gathering, you may actually do yourself a disservice and miss some valid points that could in fact help you with a problem you have.

Your social agenda is jam-packed between the

23rd and 26th. You may even need a social secretary to keep up with all the letters, phone calls, e-mails and other forms of communication. As long as you have a careful game plan, you are likely to enjoy this period, but remember to balance your fun times with rest as well.

After the 29th you may opt to take some time out and generally allow yourself to be lazy. You might feel as though you need some sort of approval from a friend, which could cause you to see them in a rather negative light. Don't probe for compliments; allow them to be offered freely.

Work and money

On or about the 6th some sort of confrontation is likely, which is because you'd rather talk than listen. You need to be a team player at this time otherwise you could get other people's backs up. You need to consult others for their expertise now and not pretend you know something that you don't.

The period of the 7th to the 10th is important for highlighting those areas in your professional activities that are not to your liking. Make that appointment with your employer, your group manager or other significant superiors so that you can effect some change. If you don't speak up now you may have to put up with these problems for much longer.

Your sense of purpose and goal orientation is very clear from the 16th. You may achieve some ambition you've been slowly but surely working on for sometime. Things are coming into focus, that's for sure, and it is an opportunity to get what you want in life. However, don't stop until the bigger goal is reached.

New contacts in your workplace can actually act as wonderful mentors to help you see the possibilities that previously were not evident to you. This is a great way to recognise your worth clearly. Up to this point you may have actually been underestimating your capacity and value.

Up till the 30th you have the opportunity to change direction and create a better course in life for yourself professionally.

Destiny dates

Positive: 1, 2, 3, 4, 5, 11, 12, 14, 16, 17, 19, 20, 24, 25, 27, 28, 29, 30

Negative: 13, 18

Mixed: 6, 7, 8, 9, 10, 21, 22, 23, 26

Highlights of the month

Your clear thinking can lift any fog that is lingering in your mind between the 2nd and the 4th. A decision is exciting now and will be profitable in future.

Between the 5th and the 7th, you'll appreciate your own talents much more. Remember that self-love doesn't necessarily mean your ego or vanity is getting the better of you. You can appreciate and enjoy the goodness in yourself without feeling guilty about it.

Your observations are first rate between the 8th and the 12th; however, by the same token, you may see something that is hard to fathom or accept. Friendships may turn around as a result. Be honest and speak your mind, even if others make it hard for you to do so.

You can discover an intense emotional attach-ment between the 13th and the 18th, which could be to someone whom you least expect. You'll be busy managing your feelings. You mustn't be pushy in love, nor should you let someone else push you over the edge.

Sometime between the 22nd and the 25th, friendships are likely to start changing. This will be a spring cleaning of sorts; a time when the old saying, 'out with the old and in with the new' will seem very appropriate to you. Naturally you may feel a little saddened that you'll have to move forward alone, but it is for the best and, the moment you do, you'll create a brand new space around you that attracts a whole range of different characters into your life.

Between the 27th and the 29th, you can expect improved communications in your workplace. Your managers and co-workers will appreciate what you have to say. Develop your powers of speech and language even more because this is a valuable asset that will hold you in good stead down the track.

Mars and Saturn are not comfortable in each other's company, and this will be reflected in some severity and harshness that is directed both from, and to, you. Someone may not approve of your actions, which could result in considerable frustration.

The reverse is also true and you may be demanding that someone change their ways. However, if you analyse the situation carefully, you'll realise you're probably exaggerating and that your motivation is quite likely based upon your own ego.

Romance and friendship

Between the 2nd and 5th you may feel completely sandwiched between the right thing to do and other people's opinions and demands. You may see something that needs rectifying but will be worried you will tread on other people's toes by doing so. This is all about how you package the help you offer. If you are diplomatic enough you will please everyone ... on this one point, at least.

You could be taken aback around the 7th when someone offers to help you with your plans. You might be suspicious at first; but keep in mind that the activity or the event you have in mind may be an opportunity for them to learn, to grow and receive some of your wisdom in the process. Share your knowledge with a friend.

You'll be extremely independent after the 9th, and this is good, unless of course you are in a relationship with someone who is feeling insecure at this time. Because you want to assert yourself openly, dramatically and without opposition, you might be insensitive to the needs of your significant other. By all means carve out that independent space for yourself if need be, but don't leave your loved ones languishing by the side of the highway of life.

Share the power and the glory you'll receive from being charming, magnetic and appealing between the 12th and the 15th. This is because, if you are with your usual peer group and find yourself attracting more attention than the others, this could backfire and create some sort of envy. Try to approach your social life with a more inclusive attitude so that others benefit from your popularity as well.

Don't go bottling up your feelings between the 18th and the 25th. That's not a good idea at all, especially given the conjoining of Mars and Saturn in the uppermost part of your horoscope. This combination will affect your personal life and make you somewhat uncomfortable and dissatisfied, for no apparent reason. Remember to develop the 'attitude of gratitude' during this cycle because it will be easy to find fault with yourself and others.

In the last couple of days of the month, particularly on the 30th, you'll notice an upswing in your social appetite. You may hear news from several different people asking you to be part of their social scene.

Work and money

The combined influence of Jupiter and Uranus is extremely lucky and shows you are prepared to think outside the square during the month of July. From the 2nd until the 4th there are wonderful opportunities when you can provide some clues to developing business and professional ideas. Your superiors will be keenly interested in implementing what you have to offer, so don't be shy in coming forward.

With the entry of Venus to your zone of career on the 10th you'd have to say that this is probably one of the most important periods of the year for your professional popularity. Although you have the tense relationship of Mars and Saturn, the influence of Venus will soften the blow and in fact make this a very lucky period for you.

Your employers will be looking after you and will notice the good work you are doing. Perhaps this is the perfect opportunity to ask them for improved working conditions and a pay rise, if you are bold enough!

After the 23rd, try to be more consistent at work. It may be a period where you want to achieve huge amounts in a small amount of time, only to find yourself lacking in energy to complete the task. Slow and steady certainly wins the race.

Destiny dates

Positive: 6, 7, 8, 9, 10, 11, 12, 13, 14, 15, 16, 17, 27, 28, 29, 30

Negative: 19, 20, 21

Mixed: 2, 3, 4, 5, 18, 22, 23, 24, 25

Highlights of the month

During this phase of your life you will improve your relationships by going back in time to weed out those unsavoury experiences that have been holding you back. Anything that has scarred you emotionally will need to be dealt with, firstly by recognising what those problems are, and then by honestly accepting your part in those chapters of your life by taking full responsibility. You'll be so surprised at what a difference this will make in not further sabotaging any existing, or new, relationships.

Extravagance seems to be rampant between the 2nd and the 5th and, by being so overconfident, it may be too late to make amends by the time the bubble bursts. Keep a tight rein on your expenses during the first few days of the month.

Venus is excellent for you between the 6th and the 9th, indicating new friends, lots of fun and enjoyable amusements, parties and generally great company. Have a few laughs to try to forget about any of the day-to-day worries that have been hounding you.

Love can cool a little between the 10th and the 13th, making you feel distant and causing your feelings to be suppressed. Both friends and lovers are not as approachable as usual, which could make you switch off as well. Keep the lines of communication open.

During this same cycle, you'll need to be a little thriftier with money, but this may be more to do with a demand being placed on you by your spouse or partner.

From the 14th till the 17th, some unexpected event may occur within your domestic sphere and you'll have absolutely no control over it, so what good will worrying do? My suggestion for you is to step back a little and let the drama unfold. Once the dust settles, then perhaps you may be able to steer what's left of the situation in the right direction.

From the 19th to the 21st, you must let someone else make their own decision, even if you feel as if you know better. You mustn't take on their responsibility. They need to learn how to do something for themselves.

You'll have a strong desire to sign contracts and to negotiate some new venture or business plan between the 21st and the 28th. Even those of you who are not involved in business per se must be careful not to accept the terms and conditions that are placed on you by someone else, even if it happens to be the local gardener or a cleaner coming to do some work for you at your home. Wait until you investigate matters more thoroughly.

Between the 30th and the 31st you'll have much more power in your work and this will cause you to create some new pathways. Money will be on the increase and therefore the last few days of August should generally be quite fulfilling for you.

For singles, it's not a bad idea to give yourself permission to seek out alternative environments and people, to give you a taste of how others live and behave. Yet again for you, the learning curve continues and may even get quite steep during this month.

Romance and friendship

You'll probably feel quite guilty during August because you realise you need to step away from a friendship that may have been with you for years. Why the guilt? Just accept that people come for a reason, stay for a while, and then often have to part ways with you. That's the way of life and you shouldn't try to hold on to things that have outlived their usefulness—including relationships.

Between the 5th and 9th much of your attention will be on resolving differences you have with your social group or a friend in particular. Call a spade a spade and don't make any apologies for being forthright and completely transparent.

Once again unexpected events in your home can turn your life upside down, particularly between the 14th and 18th. You need to make sure you understand what everyone else's agenda is, otherwise you might not be useful to the group, even if you are organised with your own diary and timetables. Get everyone on the same page and synchronise the group's activities. This will create a much more streamlined day-to-day existence in your family life.

Passion runs wild after the 21st due to the conjunction of Venus and Mars. Lust takes precedence over love, so be careful.

Mixed communications could create more work for you emotionally than is necessary after the 24th. Ask the question and rephrase it if you are not completely certain of the intention or meaning. Shortcut your way to happiness through clear and concise communications.

The month ends on a high note with the Moon conjoining Uranus in your fourth house. After the 28th a family get-together or an impromptu party with friends and neighbours will help release quite a bit of tension and decompress any of the strained relations you previously have had with relatives.

Work and money

You'll be throwing yourself into your work but from the 1st to the 5th your employer could be standing behind you with the whip, making you do things you aren't happy about. This is the price you have to pay for success.

You continue to be more frugal and economical, especially during the conjunction of Venus and Saturn in your eleventh zone of profits after the 9th. This continues up until the 13th when you realise that, while it's not impossible to save, it does actually require a bit of sacrifice on your part.

You can lavish some gifts on others around the 14th. Even though this costs a bit of money, you'll see the emotional benefits far outweighing any of the material gains that can be had by saving that money.

If someone owes you money, you may have to put your foot down between the 20th and 23rd. Make no apologies for making them keep their word. You work hard for your money and there's no reason for you to be short-changed by anyone.

Personal health matters could be related to work around the 30th. Make sure your health insurance, workers' compensation scheme or other term payments are up to date.

Destiny dates

Positive: 6, 7, 8, 31

Negative: 1, 2, 3, 4, 5

Mixed: 10, 11, 12, 13, 14, 15, 16, 17, 18, 19, 20, 21, 22, 23, 24, 25, 26, 27, 28, 30

SEPTEMBER

Highlights of the month

Your negotiations may seem promising between the 3rd and the 5th; but keep in mind this may be only the tip of the iceberg. What lurks beneath the surface may not be all that it seems. Ask questions, and even more questions, to get to the truth.

From the 6th to the 10th, you'll be extremely idealistic in your love affairs, but don't fall into the trap of believing something is better than it is. And, what's more, impulsive one-night stands and love affairs seldom last. Check the credentials of your lovers first. There should be no embarrassment in seeking to understand the person before giving more of yourself to them.

On the 13th, it's full-steam ahead on projects, with contracts and other verbal agreements now getting the green light. You'll be able to cast aside any indecision and can expect a good outcome as a result.

Your energy is on the wane between the 14th and the 18th due to the transit of Mars in your twelfth zone of secrets and low-key affairs. Rest. Get a full medical check-up if you don't feel well. It may also be time for you to get some dental work done. Psychology and other spiritual studies will help you rejuvenate your spiritual self.

Between the 19th and the 25th, there's a lucky streak apparent and you might do well to buy a lottery ticket or scratchy to see just how much karma there is in store for you. It's under transits like this that you may win something, and even if it's not a huge amount, it will still be fun, won't it?

From the 26th to the 30th, you'll be feeling quite wilful and odd in your personality. You're likely to do something drastic that friends may not appreciate. Generally, this period will prove to be one in which you are unpredictable and the affairs of life equally unexpected. You should be a little more prepared in your planning and don't leave too much to chance. This way, you won't be surprised when things don't go quite as you had anticipated.

Romance and friendship

Between the 1st and 3rd you may find yourself in a situation where you lose control of yourself. This could be due to peer pressure or taking your eye off the ball ethically, so to speak. It will take inner strength to stick to your guns morally and not be swayed by public opinion.

Between the 8th and the 9th, be careful not to let your imagination get the better of you. It's quite likely you'll be tired, bored or simply wanting some change from the routine of day-to-day existence. Rather than worrying about what is wrong with your life and relationships, try to focus on the creative aspects of your life—your talents and what is required to make you a better person—to improve your experiences.

Transformations in your personality are likely to come about after the 10th. Venus, the planet of love, moves through your zone of spiritual enlightenment and ensures that you gain some special new insights into what is necessary to make your love life more playful and enjoyable. This transit can evoke many deep and primal instincts.

At this time you'll also have the opportunity to express your compassionate and humanitarian side. Between the 11th and 13th there are opportunities for you to do some community service and relieve some suffering in the world.

Sometime between the 15th and 19th you will have some concern for your family. This isn't a bad thing, but perhaps you realise you have too much on your plate at this moment to deal with these emotions, which ironically could relate to the organisation of a dinner or reunion. You mustn't shoulder the burden of the whole responsibility but rather delegate tasks to other people. You're likely to play the martyr right now, much to your own dismay.

If you're not organised around the 23rd you may have to make some last-minute changes due to some unanticipated letdowns by others. Make sure you have checked and double-checked the arrangements and made those calls to friends to get their commitment to the engagement.

There is no way to turn back the hands of the clock but around the 28th you have the opportunity to reconnect with old friends and relive some of those great memories you have shared. Journeys to distant places or to old school events or reunions can be a lot of fun but also make you realise just how quickly time flies by.

Work and money

Your mind is extremely sharp this month due to the combined influence of the Sun and Mercury on your working life. You'll be able to retain details and information and are prone to learning all sorts of facts and figures.

Sharing this information with others will be beneficial because they'll also be prepared to divulge new techniques and methodologies to you. Because of this, any type of sales, teaching, negotiation and business interaction is positive for you. Take full advantage of these energies, particularly around the 6th to the 8th.

Between the 10th and 16th, make sure you have all the information you need on the tip of your tongue and be ready to deliver it when the moment arises. Clear and articulate communication will be a strong focus during this cycle and will help you to deliver the goods, so to speak.

Although your work and finances are set to improve there could be a glitch in your approach to dealing with superiors after the 23rd. Try not to one-up your employer or co-workers because you are likely to be at odds with their opinions, even if what you have to say is correct on every point. Your ideas will be strong but your tendency to sideswipe them is also likely.

Destiny dates

Positive: 6, 7, 8, 10, 11, 12, 13, 20, 21, 22, 24, 25
Negative: 1, 2, 26, 27, 29, 30
Mixed: 3, 4, 5, 9, 10, 14, 15, 16, 17, 18, 19, 23

Highlights of the month

From the 1st to the 4th, your responsibilities weigh heavily upon you and you mustn't make any commitment you can't keep. You must first be honest with yourself before you can be honest with others, so if you know in your heart of hearts that you can't deliver, don't say 'yes'.

Your mind is completely scattered between the 5th and the 7th and this is due to the combined influence of Uranus and Mercury. These two planets activate your restlessness and make it hard for you to concentrate or achieve any lasting results in your work.

Speak with friends between the 8th and 11th because they can open new doors and help you connect with an alternative network of people. This has equal value socially as much as commercially. This is a time when you can mix a little business with pleasure.

At the same time a brother or sister may need

some assistance, so try to give them at least a little bit of your time during their period of need. You could also reconnect with someone from your past—an acquaintance, an old school friend or just someone from your old peer group—who just happens to reappear out of nowhere.

Between the 12th and the 14th, a lover or close friend exits stage left and may disappear for a while or at least be scarce and stop calling. Be patient and allow them the space they need to go through what they're going through.

You may be forced to make a journey or travel for some unpleasant reason between the 16th and the 19th. This may be a family issue and it's quite likely unavoidable. Do the best with the resources and abilities that are at your disposal.

You can be very dynamic and want the world to know it between the 22nd and the 25th. A desire to try something new or challenging will be scratching away at you. You will grow mentally during this period but may feel a bit impatient with others who are not quite as motivated or mentally exciting.

A letter or phone call will stimulate you between the 26th and the 30th. Your passion is to experience more but you may not be completely clear on what you want. You mustn't play mind games with others but rather should sidestep anyone whom you know isn't being straightforward with you.

Romance and friendship

You'll have to deal with some news relating to a relative who may be having problems in their relationships between the 5th and 7th. It could be news of a separation or divorce, the cause of which reminds you of your own situation. This event could give you some food for thought and a wake-up call if you've become lazy in dealing with similar matters in your own life.

Your personality and that of a friend may be at odds between the 8th and 11th. Simply accept the fact that there are differences between you and each can't force the other to be a clone. Don't lose it over conflicting opinions.

A friend who is thoroughly sick and tired of giving their all to someone they love may lean on you for some advice between the 12th and 18th. However, your advice seems to be falling on deaf ears and you could find yourself reaching a point of severe frustration. You must realise that sometimes people have to experience their own difficulties to learn their karmic lessons.

Around the 23rd your most significant other, such as a spouse or long-term lover, may reveal something to you about what's going on in their world. If there are blind spots in your relationship and you haven't been altogether aware of what happens in their work or personal social life, this will be an eye-opener for you. Remember that reinventing your relationships takes a lot of time and effort.

Be prepared to pay additional attention to your loved ones and friends between the 25th and 31st. You realise that things are meant to improve but only if you put in the prerequisite energy. You'll be spending considerable time looking at new perspectives and ways of propelling your love life forward. This is the time to get out and about in a bookshop and pick up some of those self-help, pop psychology or relationship rescue books that are on the shelves. You'll be ready for and receptive to what's on offer.

Work and money

You can gain through another person's loss around the 4th. By this I mean that if you are in the right position professionally when someone exits quickly, it could be time for you to step into their shoes. Don't forget, however, that this may be a tall order and you need to be reasonably confident you are up to the task and able to fulfil the role as adequately as the person who will no longer be there.

Your key words between the 7th and 10th are frugality, seriousness and concentrated work practices. Things are likely to occur slowly and you mustn't push for fast results. The prevailing trends demand that you act more slowly and deliberately to get the best possible results.

Between the 12th and the 15th you'll be focused on setting aside money for a rainy day so you'll be able to weather the storm of uncertain financial times. You can be progressive without being speculative. Study up on new ways to make money and to save as well.

Between the 23rd and 28th, you need to draw a line in the sand and set parameters as to what time you are going to allocate to work, and what time you'll allocate to recreation, rest and quality moments with the ones you love. This will be a period where you are trying to create greater harmony between these important facets of your life.

Destiny dates

Positive: 22, 29, 30, 31

Negative: 1, 2, 11

Mixed: 4, 5, 6, 7, 8, 9, 10, 12, 13, 14, 15, 16, 17, 18, 23, 24, 25, 26, 27, 28

Highlights of the month

You have some difficult choices in November when Venus, which has a strong bearing on your friendships, moves into a compromising position whereby you may need to refuse the requests of someone to help them financially. There may be other forms of compromise as well, for example, you may be requested to keep a secret that might go against your moral fibre.

You must trust your intuition in that moment and not rely on book knowledge or past religious standards to come to your conclusion. If you are unable to meet the needs of this friend, Saturn certainly indicates that you may have to part ways permanently. This could be the issue that was raised earlier in the year and now comes back for its final resolution.

There's nothing worse than feeling obscure or unnoticed. Between the 1st and the 4th, you may feel a little under the weather in this respect.

However, you mustn't for a minute assume that if you're not invited to some function, it's because you've done something wrong. The reasons may not be clear immediately, but don't beat yourself up over it. This cycle will pass fairly quickly and things will get back to normal.

You may not have too much of an inclination to work during this same period. Spending time with yourself seems more attractive than being with others. Spiritual strength can be gained just now, so take it as a lesson to improve the inner part of your character.

You're lucky in your communications between the 5th and the 9th and should get some sort of good break. This is a favourable time for meetings, interviews or other important get-togethers. Rather than speaking too much, let your magnetic personality do the talking for you.

The 10th to the 14th brings to you several romantic opportunities. Even if you're married, the two of you can restate your love for each other. Why not do that by taking off to a romantic getaway, which will be great for your relationship?

During the period of the 18th to the 25th, Mars dominates you but also endangers you at the same time. Watch your step. Drive carefully and don't argue over trifles with others. No good will come of it. It's best to avoid arguments, even though you have the upper hand. It takes more control to hold back than to let fly!

Jealousy should be completely rooted out between the 26th and the 30th. Even if you think that what you're saying isn't exactly possessive, others will take it that way. On the contrary, be generous and give others their freedom. They will come back to you eventually, and this way you'll know that being with you hasn't been forced upon them.

Romance and friendship

You will finetune your correspondence skills between the 1st and 4th, which will involve discussing some abstract or philosophical ideas. This is a great mental exercise but can also further cement your friendships with people near and far.

On the 6th and 7th self-control is absolutely necessary and working with older people means you can learn about others and yourself. At first you may feel inferior about how much they know, but don't forget you are younger, and that is par for the course.

On the 8th, spontaneous actions will certainly allow you to let off considerable emotional steam, but you may irritate others in the process. Keep a lid on it.

Between the 9th and 13th you could be nervous about meeting someone; maybe a romantic possibility? You can try to give your emotions free rein, but unfortunately you might also still feel uncomfortable until you get to know the person better.

On the 14th and 15th pleasant moods characterise these days, and contacts with women in particular will give you a feeling of connectedness.

On the 19th both Jupiter and Venus move in their direct motion, which is an astrological go-ahead for you to implement your ideas, irrespective of what others think or feel about them. This is a period of moral certitude and makes you feel comfortable with the decisions you make.

Between the 21st and 23rd you should quickly resolve any outstanding issues. If you procrastinate you will miss the boat and, because you are so restless, it is important for you to move into the new year with a clean slate, having cleared any emotional baggage out of the picture. You will be quite impatient to get your message across, that's for sure.

From the 25th to 29th, go out and purchase jewellery, clothing and other fashion accessories that will make you shine in the crowd. You want to be noticed and loved, but by the same token, remember you also have the chance to pick up a bargain or two after the Christmas rush is over.

Work and money

Between the 2nd and 8th you mustn't let others dictate how to do your work. You should stand firm on your ideas and principles knowing full well you have the experience and the desire to do your work in a way that befits you.

From the 10th to the 15th it's a good idea to relax in your role. Overcoming tensions means more productivity and this will be a period when you can achieve a lot.

A co-worker may become much friendlier than you expect between the 17th and 22nd. Do they have some ulterior motive? Probably not, but it's best to remain cautious.

Between the 26th and 30th there could be a conflict of interests in your business affairs. You may sense some hidden agenda, so tread warily.

Destiny dates

Positive: 14, 15, 17

Negative: 24

Mixed: 1, 2, 3, 4, 5, 6, 7, 8, 9, 10, 11, 12, 13, 18, 19, 20, 21, 22, 23, 25, 26, 27, 28, 29, 30

Highlights of the month

Between the 1st and the 5th, money concerns will overwhelm you. You may not have the time to manage them all, so why not get some help? You need to delegate some of the financial tasks, especially if you're trying to make heads or tails of a taxation requirement.

From the 6th to the 8th your energy is again high and physical exercise is not a bad idea. Why not sign up for a new gym membership? Are you aware that some health funds even allow you to make a claim against this type of expense? Look into that. You can kill two birds with one stone, those being financial savings and improved health.

You must check and recheck your statements between the 10th and the 14th. There may be errors you've overlooked, but these can actually work in your favour. You'll find yourself with a healthier bank balance once you identify where those errors are.

The period leading up to Christmas, particularly between the 15th and the 19th, may be full of tension. Try to decompress the family situation rather than inflaming it with your opinions. Why not act as a peacemaker rather than a troublemaker during this festive season?

Lunar and solar eclipses are some of the most important astrological developments this month. With the powerful lunar eclipse occurring on the 21st, it will grill you to sort out any lingering marital or romantic problems. Certain revelations may be hard to stomach, but once these surface and are removed from the picture, your relationship will be so much better.

Mercury excites you between the 22nd and the 30th. Your love of travel and adventure means that you'll have to get away, feeling it's necessary to finish the year with an escape to a beautiful and peaceful location. What a wonderful way to conclude 2010!

Romance and friendship

Between the 2nd and 6th a sense of duty to your family causes you to sidestep social offers. In any case, you'll prefer your own company so it's not a bad idea to just lay low for a while until your energy is back on track.

Between the 7th and 10th, learning about your family history, your genealogy, is an advantage because it will help you to understand yourself. You'll find photographs, notebooks and other family paraphernalia fascinating.

Neighbours in this period may act strangely, but it's best for you to bite your tongue for the sake of peace.

From the 14th to the 20th it's not a bad idea to make a show of your strength without pouncing. Flexing your muscles to avoid a future problem is a wise move. Children will need directing, and vehicles and other entertainment items may need to be fairly shared, which can also present its own set of problems inasmuch as who gets what and when.

Between the 24th and 30th Christmas will be enjoyable with numerous friends and lots of fun. Older members of the community cross your path and befriending them will make you feel less stressful for some strange reason. Enjoy the closing part of 2010 fully!

Work and money

Between the 5th and 10th finish off negotiations and don't create any more work for yourself. Prepare for some well-deserved time off.

Mercury and Pluto indicate that you may want to make money or prestige a reason for an argument with someone between the 14th and 20th. That's not a particularly good idea. Show what you can do, not what you have. Trying to impress others with your wealth will not work and may in fact go against your best interests.

The eclipse of the 21st occurs in your partnership sector and indicates that you want a more diverse arrangement in your work, particularly with colleagues. Make it happen!

Between the 28th and 30th, expect extra profits to flow in. This providence will be a nice bonus to finish 2010!

Destiny dates

Positive: 22, 23, 24, 25, 26, 27, 28, 29, 30

Negative: 1

Mixed: 2, 3, 4, 5, 6, 10, 11, 12, 13, 14, 15, 16, 17, 18, 19, 20, 21

SAGITTARIUS

2010:
Astronumerology

> *Success is not the key to happiness. Happiness is the key to success. If you love what you are doing, you will be successful.*

—Herman Cain

The power behind your name

By adding the numbers of your name you can see which planet is ruling you. Each of the letters of the alphabet is assigned a number, which is listed below. These numbers are ruled by the planets. This is according to the ancient Chaldean system of numerology and is very different to the Pythagorean system to which many refer.

Each number is assigned a planet:

AIQJY	=	1	**Sun**
BKR	=	2	**Moon**
CGLS	=	3	**Jupiter**
DMT	=	4	**Uranus**
EHNX	=	5	**Mercury**
UVW	=	6	**Venus**
OZ	=	7	**Neptune**
FP	=	8	**Saturn**
—	=	9	**Mars**

Notice that the number 9 is not aligned with a letter because it is considered special. Once the numbers have been added you will see that a single planet rules your name and personal affairs. Many famous actors, writers and musicians change their names to attract the energy of a luckier planet. You can experiment with the list and try new names or add the letters of your second name to see how that vibration suits you. It's a lot of fun!

Here is an example of how to find out the power of your name. If your name is John Smith, calculate the ruling planet by assigning each letter to a number in the table like this:

J O H N S M I T H
1 7 5 5 3 4 1 4 5

Now add the numbers like this:
$1 + 7 + 5 + 5 + 3 + 4 + 1 + 4 + 5 = 35$
Then add $3 + 5 = 8$

The ruling number of John Smith's name is 8, which is ruled by Saturn. Now study the name-number table to reveal the power of your name. The numbers 3 and 5 will also play a secondary role in John's character and destiny, so in this case you would also study the effects of Jupiter and Mercury.

Name-number table

Your name number	Ruling planet	Your name characteristics
1	Sun	Magnetic individual. Great energy and life force. Physically dynamic and sociable. Attracts good friends and individuals in powerful positions. Good government connections. Intelligent, impressive, flashy and victorious. A loyal number for relationships.
2	Moon	Soft, emotional nature. Changeable moods but psychic, intuitive senses. Imaginative nature and empathetic expression of feelings. Loves family, mother and home life. Night owl who probably needs more sleep. Success with the public and/or women.
3	Jupiter	Outgoing, optimistic number with lucky overtones. Attracts opportunities without trying. Good sense of timing. Religious or spiritual aspirations.

Your name number	Ruling planet	Your name characteristics
		Can investigate the meaning of life. Loves to travel and explore the world and people.
4	Uranus	Explosive character with many unusual aspects. Likes the untried and novel. Forward thinking, with many extraordinary friends. Gets fed up easily so needs plenty of invigorating experiences. Pioneering, technological and imaginative. Wilful and stubborn when wants to be. Unexpected events in life may be positive or negative.
5	Mercury	Quick-thinking mind with great powers of speech. Extremely vigorous life; always on the go and lives on nervous energy. Youthful attitude and never grows old. Looks younger than actual age. Young friends and humorous disposition. Loves reading and writing.
6	Venus	Delightful personality. Graceful and attractive character who cherishes friends

Your name number	Ruling planet	Your name characteristics
		and social life. Musical or artistic interests. Good for money making as well as abundant love affairs. Career in the public eye is possible. Loves family but is often overly concerned by friends.
7	**Neptune**	Intuitive, spiritual and self-sacrificing nature. Easily misled by those who need help. Loves to dream of life's possibilities. Has curative powers. Dreams are revealing and prophetic. Loves the water and will have many journeys in life. Spiritual aspirations dominate worldly desires.
8	**Saturn**	Hard-working, focused individual with slow but certain success. Incredible concentration and self-sacrifice for a goal.
		Money orientated but generous when trust is gained. Professional but may be a hard taskmaster. Demands

highest standards and needs to learn to enjoy life a little more.

9	**Mars**	Fantastic physical drive and ambition. Sports and outdoor activities are keys to wellbeing. Confrontational. Likes to work and play just as hard. Caring and protective of family, friends and territory. Individual tastes in life but is also self-absorbed. Needs to listen to others' advice to gain greater success.

Your 2010 planetary ruler

Astrology and numerology are very intimately connected. As already shown, each planet rules over a number between 1 and 9. Both your name *and* your birth date are ruled by planetary energies.

Add the numbers of your birth date and the year in question to find out which planet will control the coming year for you.

For example, if you were born on the 12th of November, add the numerals 1 and 2 (12, your day of birth) and 1 and 1 (11, your month of birth) to the year in question, in this case 2010 (the current year), like this:

$1 + 2 + 1 + 1 + 2 + 0 + 1 + 0 = 8$

The planet ruling your individual karma for 2010 will be Saturn because this planet rules the number 8.

You can even take your ruling name-number as shown earlier and add it to the year in question to throw more light on your coming personal affairs, like this:

John Smith = 8

Year coming = 2010

8 + 2 + 0 + 1 + 0 = 11

1 + 1 = 2

Therefore, 2 is the ruling number of the combined name and date vibrations. Study the Moon's number 2 influence for 2010.

Outlines of the year number ruled by each planet are given below. Enjoy!

1 is the year of the Sun

Overview

The Sun is the brightest object in the heavens and rules number 1 and the sign of Leo. Because of this the coming year will bring you great success and popularity.

You'll be full of life and radiant vibrations and are more than ready to tackle your new nine-year cycle, which begins now. Any new projects you commence are likely to be successful.

Your health and vitality will be very strong and your stamina at its peak. Even if you happen to have the odd problem with your health, your recuperative power will be strong.

You have tremendous magnetism this year so social popularity won't be a problem for you. I see many new friends and lovers coming into your life. Expect loads of invitations to parties and fun-filled outings. Just don't take your health for granted as you're likely to burn the candle at both ends.

With success coming your way, don't let it go to your head. You must maintain humility, which will make you even more popular in the coming year.

Love and pleasure

This is an important cycle for renewing your love and connections with your family, particularly if you have children. The Sun is connected with the sign of Leo and therefore brings an increase in musical and theatrical activities. Entertainment and other creative hobbies will be high on your agenda and bring you a great sense of satisfaction.

Work

You won't have to make too much of an effort to be successful this year because the brightness of the Sun will draw opportunities to you. Changes in work are likely and, if you have been concerned that opportunities are few and far between, 2010 will be different. You can expect some sort of promotion or an increase in income because your employers will take special note of your skills and service orientation.

Improving your luck

Leo is the ruler of number 1 and, therefore, if you're born under this star sign, 2010 will be particularly lucky. For others, July and August, the months of Leo, will bring good fortune. The 1st, 8th, 15th and 22nd hours of Sundays especially will give you a unique sort of luck in any sort of competition or activities generally. Keep your eye out for those born under Leo as they may be able to contribute something to your life and may even have a karmic connection to you. This is a particularly important year for your destiny.

Your lucky numbers in this coming cycle are 1, 10, 19 and 28.

2 is the year of the Moon

Overview

There's nothing more soothing than the cool light of the full Moon on a clear night. The Moon is emotional and receptive and controls your destiny in 2010. If you're able to use the positive energies of the Moon, it will be a great year in which you can realign and improve your relationships, particularly with family members.

Making a commitment to becoming a better person and bringing your emotions under control will also dominate your thinking. Try not to let your emotions get the better of you throughout the coming year because you may be drawn into the changeable nature of these lunar vibrations as well. If you fail to keep control of your emotional life you'll later regret some of your actions. You must blend careful thinking with feeling to arrive at the best results. Your luck throughout 2010 will certainly be determined by the state of your mind.

Because the Moon and the sign of Cancer rule the number 2 there is a certain amount of change to be expected this year. Keep your feelings steady and don't let your heart rule your head.

Love and pleasure

Your primary concern in 2010 will be your home and family life. You'll be finally keen to take on those renovations, or work on your garden. You may even think of buying a new home. You can at last carry out some of those plans and make your dreams come true. If you find yourself a little more temperamental than usual, do some extra meditation and spend time alone until you sort this out. You mustn't withhold your feelings from your partner as this will only create frustration.

Work

During 2010 your focus will be primarily on feelings and family; however, this doesn't mean you can't make great strides in your work as well. The Moon rules the general public and what you might find is that special opportunities and connections with the world at large present themselves to you. You could be working with large numbers of people.

If you're looking for a better work opportunity, try to focus your attention on women who can give you a hand. Use your intuition as it will be finely tuned this year. Work and career success depends upon your instincts.

Improving your luck

The sign of Cancer is your ruler this year and because the Moon rules Mondays, both this day of the week and the month of July are extremely lucky for you. The 1st, 8th, 15th and 22nd hours on Mondays will be very powerful. Pay special attention to the new and full Moon days throughout 2010.

The numbers 2, 11 and 29 are lucky for you.

3 is the year of Jupiter

Overview

The year 2010 will be a number 3 year for you and, because of this, Jupiter and Sagittarius will dominate your affairs. This is extremely lucky and shows you'll be motivated to broaden your horizons, gain more money and become extremely popular in your social circles. It looks like 2010 will be a fun-filled year with much excitement.

Jupiter and Sagittarius are generous to a fault and so, likewise, your open-handedness will mark the year. You'll be friendly and helpful to all of those around you.

Pisces is also under the rulership of the number 3 and this brings out your spiritual and compassionate nature. You'll become a much better person, reducing your negative karma by increasing your self-awareness and spiritual feelings. You will want to share your luck with those you love.

Love and pleasure

Travel and seeking new adventures will be part and parcel of your romantic life this year. Travelling to distant lands and meeting unusual people will open your heart to fresh possibilities of romance.

You'll try novel and audacious things and will find yourself in a different circle of friends. Compromise will be important in making your existing relationships work. Talk about your feelings. If you are currently in a relationship you'll feel an upswing in your affection for your partner. This is a perfect opportunity to deepen your love for each other and take your relationship to a new level.

If you're not yet attached to someone, there's good news for you. Great opportunities lie in store and a spiritual or karmic connection may be experienced in 2010.

Work

Great fortune can be expected through your working life in the next twelve months. Your friends and work colleagues will want to help you achieve your goals. Even your employers will be amenable to your requests for extra money or a better position within the organisation.

If you want to start a new job or possibly begin an independent line of business, this is a great year to do it. Jupiter looks set to give you plenty of opportunities, success and a superior reputation.

Improving your luck

As long as you can keep a balanced view of things and not overdo anything, your luck will increase dramatically throughout 2010. The important thing is to remain grounded and not be too airy-fairy about your objectives. Be realistic about your talents and capabilities and don't brag about your skills or achievements. This will only invite envy from others.

Moderate your social life as well and don't drink or eat too much as this will slow your reflexes and weaken your chances for success.

You have plenty of spiritual insights this year so you should use them to their maximum. In the 1st, 8th, 15th and 24th hours of Thursdays you should use your intuition to enhance your luck, and the numbers 3, 12, 21 and 30 are also lucky for you. March and December are your lucky months but generally the whole year should go pretty smoothly for you.

4 is the year of Uranus

Overview

The electric and exciting planet of the zodiac, Uranus, and its sign of Aquarius, rule your affairs throughout 2010. Dramatic events will surprise and at the same time unnerve you in your professional and personal life. So be prepared!

You'll be able to achieve many things this year and your dreams are likely to come true, but you mustn't be distracted or scattered with your energies. You'll be breaking through your own self-limitations and this will present challenges from your family and friends. You'll want to be independent and develop your spiritual powers and nothing will stop you.

Try to maintain discipline and an orderly lifestyle so you can make the most of these special energies this year. If unexpected things do happen, it's not a bad idea to have an alternative plan so you don't lose momentum.

Love and pleasure

You want something radical, something different in your relationships this year. It's quite likely that your love life will be feeling a little less than exciting so you'll take some important steps to change that. If your partner is as progressive as you'll be this year, then your relationship is likely to improve and fulfil both of you.

In your social life you will meet some very unusual people, whom you'll feel are especially connected to you spiritually. You may want to ditch everything for the excitement and passion of a completely new relationship, but tread carefully as this may not work out exactly as you expect it to.

Work

Technology, computing and the Internet will play a larger role in your professional life this coming year.

You'll have to move ahead with the times and learn new skills if you want to achieve success.

A hectic schedule is likely, so make sure your diary is with you at all times. Try to be more efficient and don't waste time.

New friends and alliances at work will help you achieve even greater success in the coming period. Becoming a team player will be even more important in gaining satisfaction from your professional endeavours.

Improving your luck

Moving too quickly and impulsively will cause you problems on all fronts, so be a little more patient and think your decisions through more carefully. Social, romantic and professional opportunities will come to you but take a little time to investigate the ramifications of your actions.

The 1st, 8th, 15th and 20th hours of any Saturday are lucky, but love and luck are likely to cross your path when you least expect it. The numbers 4, 13, 22 and 31 are also lucky for you this year.

5 is the year of Mercury
Overview

The supreme planet of communication, Mercury, is your ruling planet throughout 2010. The number 5, which is connected to Mercury, will confer upon you success through your intellectual abilities.

Any form of writing or speaking will be improved and this will be, to a large extent, underpinning your success. Your imagination will be stimulated by this planet, with many incredible new and exciting ideas coming to mind.

Mercury and the number 5 are considered somewhat indecisive. Be firm in your attitude and don't let too many ideas or opportunities distract and confuse you. By all means get as much information as you can to help you make the right decisions.

I see you involved with money proposals, job applications, even contracts that need to be signed, so remain as clear-headed as possible.

Your business skills and clear and concise communication will be at the heart of your life in 2010.

Love and pleasure

Mercury, which rules the signs of Gemini and Virgo, will make your love life a little difficult due to its changeable nature. On the one hand you'll feel passionate and loving to your partner, yet on the other you will feel like giving it all up for the excitement of a new affair. Maintain the middle ground.

Also, try not to be too critical with your friends and family members. The influence of Virgo makes you prone to expecting much more from others than they're capable of giving. Control your sharp tongue and don't hurt people's feelings. Encouraging others is the better path, leading to greater emotional satisfaction.

Work

Speed will dominate your professional life in 2010. You'll be flitting from one subject to another and taking on far more than you can handle. You'll need to make some serious changes in your routine to handle the avalanche of work that will come your way. You'll also be travelling with your work, but not necessarily overseas.

If you're in a job you enjoy then this year will give you additional successes. If not, it may be time to move on.

Improving your luck

Communication is the key to attaining your desires in the coming twelve months. Keep focused on one idea rather than scattering your energies in all directions and your success will be speedier.

By looking after your health, sleeping well and exercising regularly, you'll build up your resilience and mental strength.

The 1st, 8th, 15th and 20th hours of Wednesday are lucky so it's best to schedule your meetings and other important social engagements during these times. The lucky numbers for Mercury are 5, 14, 23 and 32.

6 is the year of Venus

Overview

Because you're ruled by 6 this year, love is in the air! Venus, Taurus and Libra are well known for their affinity with romance, love, and even marriage. If ever you were going to meet a soulmate and feel comfortable in love, 2010 must surely be your year.

Taurus has a strong connection to money and practical affairs as well, so finances will also improve if you are diligent about work and security issues.

The important thing to keep in mind this year is that sharing love and making that important soul connection should be kept high on your agenda. This will be an enjoyable period in your life.

Love and pleasure

Romance is the key thing for you this year and your current relationships will become more fulfilling if you happen to be attached. For singles, a 6 year heralds an important meeting that eventually leads to marriage.

You'll also be interested in fashion, gifts, jewellery and all sorts of socialising. It's at one of these social engagements that you could meet the love of your life. Remain available!

Venus is one of the planets that has a tendency to overdo things, so be moderate in your eating and drinking. Try generally to maintain a modest lifestyle.

Work

You'll have a clearer insight into finances and your future security during a number 6 year. Whereas previously you may have had additional expenses and extra distractions, your mind will now be more settled and capable of longer-term planning along these lines.

With the extra cash you might see this year, decorating your home or office will give you a special sort of satisfaction.

Social affairs and professional activities will be strongly linked. Any sort of work-related functions may offer you romantic opportunities as well. On the other hand, be careful not to mix up your workplace relationships with romantic ideals. This could complicate some of your professional activities.

Improving your luck

You'll want more money and a life of leisure and ease in 2010. Keep working on your strengths and eliminate your negative personality traits to create greater luck and harmony in your life.

Moderate all your actions and don't focus exclusively on money and material objects. Feed your spiritual needs as well. By balancing your inner and outer sides you'll see that your romantic and professional lives will be enhanced more easily.

The 1st, 8th, 15th and 20th hours on Fridays will be very lucky for you and new opportunities will arise for you at those times. You can use the numbers 6, 15, 24 and 33 to increase luck in your general affairs.

7 is the year of Neptune

Overview

The last and most evolved sign of the zodiac is

Pisces, which is ruled by Neptune. The number 7 is deeply connected with this zodiac sign and governs you in 2010. Your ideals seem to be clearer and more spiritually orientated than ever before. Your desire to evolve and understand your inner self will be a double-edged sword. It depends on how organised you are as to how well you can use these spiritual and abstract concepts in your practical life.

Your past hurts and deep emotional issues will be dealt with and removed for good, if you are serious about becoming a better human being.

Spend a little more time caring for yourself rather than others, as it's likely some of your friends will drain you of energy with their own personal problems. Of course, you mustn't turn a blind eye to the needs of others, but don't ignore your own personal requirements in the process.

Love and pleasure

Meeting people with similar life views and spiritual aspirations will rekindle your faith in relationships. If you do choose to develop a new romance, make sure there is a clear understanding of the responsibilities of one to the other. Don't get swept off your feet by people who have ulterior motives.

Keep your relationships realistic and see that the most idealistic partnerships must eventually come down to Earth. Deal with the practicalities of life.

Work

This is a year of hard work, but one in which you'll

come to understand the deeper significance of your professional ideals. You may discover a whole new aspect to your career, which involves a more compassionate and self-sacrificing side to your personality.

You'll also find that your way of working will change and you'll be more focused and able to get into the spirit of whatever you do. Finding meaningful work is very likely and therefore this could be a year when money, security, creativity and spirituality overlap to bring you a great sense of personal satisfaction.

Tapping into your greater self through meditation and self-study will bring you great benefits throughout 2010.

Improving your luck

Using self-sacrifice along with discrimination will be an unusual method of improving your luck. The laws of karma state that what you give, you receive in greater measure. This is one of the principal themes for you in 2010.

The 1st, 8th, 15th and 20th hours of Tuesdays are your lucky times. The numbers 7, 16, 25 and 34 should be used to increase your lucky energies.

8 is the year of Saturn

Overview

The earthy and practical sign of Capricorn and its ruler Saturn are intimately linked to the number

8, which rules you in 2010. Your discipline and far-sightedness will help you achieve great things in the coming year. With cautious discernment, slowly but surely you will reach your goals.

It may be that due to the influence of the solitary Saturn, your best work and achievement will be behind closed doors away from the limelight. You mustn't fear this as you'll discover many new things about yourself. You'll learn just how strong you really are.

Love and pleasure

Work will overshadow your personal affairs in 2010, but you mustn't let this erode the personal relationships you have. Becoming a workaholic brings great material successes but will also cause you to become too insular and aloof. Your family members won't take too kindly to you working 100-hour weeks.

Responsibility is one of the key words for this number and you will therefore find yourself in a position of authority that leaves very little time for fun. Try to make the time to enjoy the company of friends and family and by all means schedule time off on the weekends as it will give you the peace of mind you're looking for.

Because of your responsible attitude it will be very hard for you not to assume a greater role in your workplace and this indicates longer working hours with the likelihood of a promotion with equally good remuneration.

Work

Money is high on your agenda in 2010. Number 8 is a good money number according to the Chinese and this year is at last likely to bring you the fruits of your hard labour. You are cautious and resourceful in all your dealings and will not waste your hard-earned savings. You will also be very conscious of using your time wisely.

You will be given more responsibilities and you're likely to take them on, if only to prove to yourself that you can handle whatever life dishes up.

Expect a promotion in which you'll play a leading role in your work. Your diligence and hard work will pay off, literally, in a bigger salary and more respect from others.

Improving your luck

Caution is one of the key characteristics of the number 8 and is linked to Capricorn. But being overly cautious could cause you to miss valuable opportunities. If an offer is put to you, try to think outside the square and balance it with your naturally cautious nature.

Be gentle and kind to yourself. By loving yourself, others will naturally love you, too. The 1st, 8th, 15th and 20th hours of Saturdays are exceptionally lucky for you, as are the numbers 1, 8, 17, 26 and 35.

9 is the year of Mars

Overview

You are now entering the final year of a nine-year cycle dominated by the planet Mars and the sign of Aries. You'll be completing many things and are determined to be successful after several years of intense work.

Some of your relationships may now have reached their use-by date and even personal affairs may need to be released. Don't let arguments and disagreements get in the road of friendly resolution in these areas of your life.

Mars is a challenging planet, and this year, although you will be very active and productive, you may find others trying to obstruct the achievement of your goals. As a result you may react strongly to them, thereby creating disharmony in your workplace. Don't be so impulsive or reckless, and generally slow things down. The slower, steadier approach has greater merit this year.

Love and pleasure

If you become too bossy and pushy with friends this year you will just end up pushing them out of your life. It's a year to end certain friendships but by the same token it could be the perfect time to remove conflicts and thereby bolster your love affairs in 2010.

If you're feeling a little irritable and angry with those you love, try getting rid of these negative feelings through some intense, rigorous sports and physical activity. This will definitely relieve tension and improve your personal life.

Work

Because you're healthy and able to work at a more intense pace you'll achieve an incredible amount in the coming year. Overwork could become a problem if you're not careful.

Because the number 9 and Mars are infused with leadership energy, you'll be asked to take the reins of the job and steer your company or group in a certain direction. This will bring with it added responsibility but also a greater sense of purpose for you.

Improving your luck

Because of the hot and restless energy of the number 9, it is important to create more mental peace in your life this year. Lower the temperature, so to speak, and decompress your relationships rather than becoming aggravated. Try to talk with your work partners and loved ones rather than telling them what to do. This will generally pick up your health and your relationships.

The 1st, 8th, 15th and 20th hours of Tuesdays are the luckiest for you this year and, if you're involved in any disputes or need to attend to health issues, these times are also very good to get the best results. Your lucky numbers are 9, 18, 27 and 36.

SAGITTARIUS

2010:
Your Daily Planner

Men are failures, not because they are stupid, but because they are not sufficiently impassioned.

—Struthers Burt

According to astrology, the success of any venture or activity is dependent upon the planetary positions at the time you commence that activity. Electional astrology helps you select the most appropriate times for many of your day-to-day endeavours. These dates are applicable to each and every zodiac sign and can be used freely by one and all, even if your star sign doesn't fall under the one mentioned in this book. Please note that the daily planner is a universal system applicable equally to all *twelve* star signs. Anyone and everyone can use this planner irrespective of their birth sign.

Ancient astrologers understood the planetary patterns and how they impacted on each of us. This allowed them to suggest the best possible times to start various important activities. For example, many farmers still use this approach today: they understand the phases of the Moon, and attest to the fact that planting seeds on certain lunar days produces a far better crop than does planting on other days.

In the following section, many facets of daily life are considered. Using the lunar cycle and the combined strength of other planets allows us to work out the best times to do them. This is your personal almanac, which can be used in conjunction with any star sign to help optimise the results.

First, select the activity you are interested in, and then quickly scan the year for the best months to start it. When you have selected the month, you can finetune your timing by finding the best specific dates. You can then be sure that the planetary energies will be in sync with you, offering you the best possible outcome.

Coupled with what you know about your monthly and weekly trends, the daily planner is an effective tool to help you capitalise on opportunities that come your way this year.

Good luck, and may the planets bless you with great success, fortune and happiness in 2010!

Getting started in 2010

How many times have you made a new year's resolution to begin a diet or be a better person in your relationships? And, how many times has it not worked out? Well, part of the reason may be that you started out at the wrong time, because how successful you are is strongly influenced by the position of the Moon and the planets when you begin a particular activity. You will be more successful with the following endeavours if you start them on the days indicated.

Relationships

We all feel more empowered on some days than on others. This is because the planets have some power over us—their movement and their relationships to each other determine the ebb and flow of our energies. And, our levels of self-confidence and sense of romantic magnetism play an important part in the way we behave in relationships.

Your daily planner tells you the ideal dates for meeting new friends, initiating a love affair, spending time with family and loved ones—it even tells you the most appropriate times for sexual encounters.

You'll be surprised at how much more impact you will make in your relationships when you tune yourself in to the planetary energies on these special dates.

Falling in love/restoring love

During these times you could expect favourable energies to meet your soulmate or, if you've had difficulty in a relationship, to approach the one you love to rekindle both your and their emotional responses:

January	18, 20, 23, 24
February	15, 16, 20, 24
March	29
April	16
May	14, 17, 18, 19, 20, 23
June	14, 15, 16, 20, 21
July	12
August	10, 13, 14
September	9, 21, 22
October	8, 18, 19, 20
November	14, 15, 16, 19, 20, 21
December	13, 17, 18

Special times with friends and family

Socialising, partying and having a good time with those whose company you enjoy is highly favourable under the following dates. They are excellent to spend time with family and loved ones in a domestic environment:

January	6, 26, 27
February	12, 13, 14, 15, 16, 20, 24
March	11, 21, 22, 29, 30, 31
April	8
May	15, 16, 17, 18, 19, 20, 23, 24
June	1, 2, 3, 11, 12, 14, 15, 16, 20, 21, 29, 30
July	8, 9, 12, 17, 18, 26, 27
August	5, 6, 9, 10, 13, 14, 22, 23, 24
September	1, 2, 5, 9, 10, 18, 19, 20, 30
October	3, 19, 20, 25, 26, 30, 31
November	3, 4, 14, 15, 16, 22, 26, 27
December	2, 9, 10, 11, 19, 20, 24, 25

Healing or resuming relationships

If you're trying to get back together with the one you love or need a heart-to-heart or deep-and-meaningful discussion with someone, you can try the following dates to do so:

January	12, 13, 14, 15, 21, 22, 23, 24, 25
February	6
March	6, 31
April	2, 7, 8, 12, 16, 19, 23, 24, 25, 26

May	10, 11, 12, 13, 14, 15, 16, 17, 18, 19, 20, 21, 22, 23, 24, 25, 26, 27, 28, 30
June	3, 8, 9, 10, 11, 12, 13, 14, 15, 16, 17, 21, 22, 23, 25, 26, 27, 28, 29, 30
July	1, 2, 3, 4, 5, 10, 11, 12, 13, 15, 16, 17, 18, 19, 20, 21, 22, 23, 28, 29, 30
August	1, 2, 3, 4, 5, 6, 9, 10, 13, 14, 15, 16, 20, 23, 25, 26, 27
September	2, 5, 9, 10, 13, 17, 18, 19, 20
October	1, 2, 3, 6, 12, 13, 14, 15, 20, 22, 23, 24, 25, 26, 27, 28, 29, 30, 31
November	3, 4, 5, 6, 7, 8, 9, 21, 27, 28, 29, 30
December	2, 3, 4, 6, 12, 13, 14, 17, 18, 19, 20, 21, 23, 24, 25

Sexual encounters

Physical and sexual energies are well favoured on the following dates. The energies of the planets enhance your moments of intimacy during these times:

January	1, 6, 7, 21, 22
February	6, 12, 13, 14, 20, 24
March	14, 15, 17, 18, 19, 30, 31
April	23, 24, 25, 26
May	9, 12, 14, 17, 18, 19, 20
June	3, 8, 9, 10, 11, 14, 15, 16, 20, 21, 29, 30
July	8, 9, 10, 11, 12
August	6, 10, 13, 14, 22, 23, 24

September	3, 4, 5, 6, 9, 10, 18, 19, 20, 21, 22, 30
October	1, 2, 3, 7, 8, 18, 19, 20, 23, 24, 28, 29, 30, 31
November	3, 4, 14, 15, 16, 19, 24, 25, 26, 27
December	2, 10, 11, 12, 13, 15, 16, 17, 19, 20, 22, 23, 24, 25

Health and wellbeing

Your aura and life force are susceptible to the movements of the planets—in particular, they respond to the phases of the Moon.

The following dates are the most appropriate times to begin a diet, have cosmetic surgery, or seek medical advice. They also indicate the best times to help others.

Feeling of wellbeing

Your physical as well as your mental alertness should be strong on these following dates. You can plan your activities and expect a good response from others:

January	2, 3, 4, 5, 6, 7, 11, 12, 13, 14, 16, 17, 18, 21, 22, 23, 24, 30, 31
February	1, 2, 7, 8, 15, 16, 17, 18, 19, 20, 21, 22, 23, 24, 25, 26, 27, 28
March	16, 17, 18, 19, 20, 22, 23, 24, 25, 26, 27, 28, 29
April	7, 13, 14, 16, 28
May	2, 11, 14, 25, 26
June	8, 22, 23, 26, 27, 28, 29, 30

July	4, 5, 8, 9, 12, 13, 14, 15, 16, 19, 20, 23, 24, 25
August	5, 6, 9, 10, 11, 12, 13, 15, 16, 20, 21
September	9, 10, 11, 12, 13, 16, 17, 21, 22, 24, 25, 28, 29, 30
October	3, 4, 5, 6, 7, 8, 9, 10, 13, 14, 15, 22
November	4, 5, 6, 10, 11, 19, 20, 21
December	7, 8, 17, 18, 28, 29

Healing and medicine

These times are good for approaching others who have expertise when you need some deeper under-standing. They are also favourable for any sort of healing or medication and making appointments with doctors or psychologists. Planning surgery around these dates should bring good results.

Often giving up our time and energy to assist others doesn't necessarily result in the expected outcome. However, by lending a helping hand to a friend on the following dates, the results should be favourable:

January	1, 2, 3, 4, 6, 7, 8, 9, 11, 12, 13, 14, 15, 16, 17, 18, 19, 20, 21, 22, 23, 24, 26, 27, 28, 29, 30, 31
February	1, 5, 6, 9, 11, 12, 13, 14, 15, 16, 19
March	1, 2, 3, 4, 5, 8, 9, 10, 11, 12, 18, 19, 24, 25, 29
April	1, 3, 4, 5, 22, 26
May	4, 5

June	1, 2, 3, 9, 10, 17, 18, 22, 23, 24, 25, 29, 30
July	6, 7, 15, 16, 17, 18, 19, 21, 22, 23, 24, 25, 26
August	2, 3, 4, 11, 12, 17, 18, 19, 20, 21, 30, 31
September	6, 7, 8, 10, 11, 12, 13, 14, 15, 16, 17, 18, 26, 27, 28, 29
October	5, 7, 8, 9, 10, 11, 12, 13, 14, 15, 16, 17, 18, 19, 20, 21, 22, 23, 24, 25, 26, 28, 29, 30, 31
November	1, 2, 3, 5, 7, 8, 10, 11, 14, 15, 17, 18, 19, 22, 23
December	4, 5, 7, 8, 9, 10, 12, 13, 14, 16, 23, 24, 25, 26, 28, 29, 30, 31

Money

Money is an important part of life, and involves many decisions—decisions about borrowing, investing, spending. The ideal times for transactions are very much influenced by the planets, and whether your investment or nest egg grows or doesn't grow can often be linked to timing. Making your decisions on the following dates could give you a whole new perspective on your financial future.

Managing wealth and money

To build your nest egg it's a good time to open your bank account or invest money on the following dates:

January	1, 6, 7, 13, 14, 15, 18, 21, 22, 28, 29
February	3, 4, 9, 10, 11, 12, 13, 14, 15, 17, 18, 24, 25
March	2, 3, 9, 10, 16, 17, 18, 23, 24, 29, 30, 31

April	5, 6, 7, 13, 14, 19, 20, 21, 26, 27,
May	2, 3, 4, 10, 11, 17, 18, 23, 24, 30, 31
June	6, 7, 8, 13, 14, 19, 20, 21, 26, 27, 28
July	4, 5, 10, 11, 12, 17, 18, 23, 24, 25, 31
August	1, 7, 8, 13, 14, 20, 21, 27, 28, 29
September	3, 4, 9, 10, 16, 17, 23, 24, 25
October	1, 2, 7, 8, 13, 14, 15, 21, 22, 28, 29
November	3, 4, 10, 11, 17, 18, 24, 25
December	1, 2, 7, 8, 14, 15, 16, 21, 22, 23, 24, 29

Spending

It's always fun to spend but the following dates are more in tune with this activity and are likely to give you better results:

January	3, 4, 5, 6, 7, 8, 9, 10, 11, 12, 13, 14
February	3, 4, 5, 10, 19
March	8, 10, 11, 13, 14, 19
April	7, 8, 11, 12, 22
May	6, 7, 8, 9, 10, 11, 12, 13, 17, 18, 19, 20, 21, 22, 23, 24, 25, 26, 27, 28
June	1, 11, 12, 14, 16, 17, 19, 23, 25, 26, 27, 28, 29, 30
July	6, 7, 8, 23, 24, 25, 26, 27, 28, 29, 31
August	1, 2, 3, 4, 5, 15, 16, 17, 18, 19, 30, 31
September	1, 2, 3, 4, 17, 18, 19, 20, 21, 22, 23, 27, 28, 29, 30
October	4, 7, 12, 13, 14, 15, 16, 17, 18, 19, 27, 28

November   2, 3, 4, 25, 26, 27, 28

December   11, 22, 23

Selling

If you're thinking of selling something, whether it is small or large, consider the following dates as ideal times to do so:

January   18

February   12, 13, 14, 15

March   5, 6, 9, 14, 15, 16, 17, 18, 19, 21

April   1, 3, 4, 5, 22, 26

May   7, 12, 21, 29

June   3, 8, 9, 10, 11, 12, 13, 17, 24, 25, 26, 27, 28, 30

July   1, 2, 7, 9, 10, 11, 25, 27, 28, 29, 30, 31

August   1, 2, 3, 4, 5, 6, 7, 8, 9, 10, 13, 20, 23, 28

September   2, 9, 10, 11, 12, 13, 14, 15, 16, 17, 18, 19, 20, 21, 22, 23, 24, 26, 30

October   1, 2, 3, 4, 6, 7, 10, 11, 17, 18, 19, 20, 21, 22, 23, 24, 25, 27, 29

November   3, 4, 5, 6, 7, 11, 14, 15, 16, 17, 18, 19, 21, 23, 24, 25, 26, 27, 28, 29, 30

December   1, 2, 3, 4, 5, 6, 7, 8, 9, 10, 11, 12, 13, 14, 15, 16, 17, 18, 19, 20, 21, 22

Borrowing

Few of us like to borrow money, but if you must, taking out a loan on the following dates will be positive:

January	12, 30
February	7, 12, 13
March	6, 7, 8, 11
April	3, 4, 8
May	9, 28, 29
June	1, 2, 3, 4, 5, 29, 30
July	1, 2, 3, 26, 27, 28, 29, 30
August	9, 25, 26
September	5, 6
October	3, 30
November	26, 27
December	3, 4, 21, 22, 23, 30, 31

Work and education

Your career is important, and continual improvement of your skills is therefore also crucial professionally, mentally and socially. The dates below will help you find out the most appropriate times to improve your professional talents and commence new work or education associated with your work.

You may need to decide when to start learning a new skill, when to ask for a promotion, and even when to make an important career change. Here are the days when your mental and educational power is strong.

Learning new skills

Educational pursuits are lucky and bring good results on the following dates:

January	15, 16, 17, 18, 19, 20, 21, 22, 25, 26, 27
February	14, 15, 16, 17, 18, 19, 22, 23, 28
March	16, 17, 18, 21, 22, 27, 28
April	17, 18, 24, 25
May	15, 16, 21, 22
June	12, 17, 18, 24, 25
July	15, 16, 21, 22, 23, 24, 25
August	11, 12, 17, 18, 19
September	8, 13, 15, 20, 21, 22
October	11, 12
November	7, 8, 9
December	6, 19, 20

Changing career path or profession

If you're feeling stuck and need to move into a new professional activity, changing jobs could be done at these times:

January	6, 7, 15, 16, 17, 23, 24
February	12, 13, 14, 19, 20, 21
March	19, 20, 27, 28
April	15, 16, 24, 25
May	14, 21, 22
June	17, 18, 19, 20, 21
July	8, 9, 15, 16, 23, 24, 25

August	5, 6, 11, 12, 20, 21, 22, 23
September	1, 2, 8, 13, 14, 15, 17
October	8, 13, 14, 15, 16, 17
November	3, 4, 10, 11, 19, 20, 21
December	1, 2, 3, 7, 8, 17, 18, 28, 29

Promotion, professional focus and hard work

To increase your mental focus and achieve good results from the work you do; promotions are also likely on these dates:

January	4, 5, 6, 11, 12, 13, 14, 15, 16, 17, 18, 19, 21
February	6
March	16, 17, 18, 19, 20, 21, 23, 24, 25, 26, 27, 28, 29
April	8, 28, 29
May	12, 21
June	25, 26, 27, 28
July	4, 5, 8, 9, 12, 13, 14, 15, 16, 17, 18, 19, 20, 21, 22, 23, 24, 25, 26, 27
August	5, 6, 10, 11, 12, 13, 14, 15, 16, 17, 18, 19, 20, 21, 22, 23, 24
September	13, 14, 15
October	10, 11, 12, 13, 14, 15, 17, 18, 19, 20, 22, 23, 24, 30, 31
November	2, 4, 5, 6, 7, 8, 9, 23, 24, 25, 26, 27, 28, 29, 30
December	2, 3, 4, 11, 12, 13, 14, 15, 16, 18, 19, 20, 21, 23, 24, 25

Travel

Setting out on a holiday or adventurous journey is exciting. Here are the most favourable times for doing this. Travel on the following dates is likely to give you a sense of fulfilment:

January	15
February	15, 16, 18, 19, 20, 21
March	16, 17, 18, 21, 22, 23
April	19, 24, 25, 26, 27
May	16, 17, 18, 21, 22
June	17, 18, 19, 20, 21, 24, 25
July	21, 22, 23, 24, 25
August	19
September	9, 21, 22
October	18, 19, 20, 21, 22
November	7, 16, 17, 18
December	6, 14, 16, 19, 20

Beauty and grooming

Believe it or not, cutting your hair or nails has a powerful effect on your body's electromagnetic energy. If you cut your hair or nails at the wrong time of the month, you can reduce your level of vitality significantly. Use these dates to ensure you optimise your energy levels by staying in tune with the stars.

Hair and nails

January   1, 2, 3, 4, 5, 6, 7, 8, 11, 12, 13, 14, 15, 18, 19, 20, 21, 22, 25, 26, 27

February   3, 4, 5, 7, 8, 15, 16, 17, 18, 19, 22, 23, 24, 25

March   2, 3, 4, 6, 7, 8, 14, 15, 21, 22

April   1, 2, 3, 4, 5, 10, 11, 12, 17, 18, 19, 20, 21, 22, 23, 28, 29, 30

May   1, 2, 3, 4, 5, 7, 8, 9, 10, 11, 12, 13, 15, 16, 17, 18, 25, 26 27, 28, 29, 30

June   4, 5, 11, 12, 14, 15, 16, 24, 25

July   1, 2, 3, 8, 9, 12, 13, 14, 21, 22, 28, 29, 30

August   1, 2, 5, 6, 17, 18, 19, 25, 26

September 1, 2, 6, 7, 14, 15, 21, 22, 23, 24, 28, 29, 30

October   3, 4, 11, 12, 18, 19, 20, 25, 26, 27, 28, 29, 30

November   7, 8, 9, 14, 15, 16, 22, 23, 24, 25, 26, 27

December   5, 6, 12, 13, 19, 20, 21, 22, 23, 24, 25

Therapies, massage and self-pampering

January   6, 7, 13, 14, 15, 18, 19, 20, 21

February   2, 3, 9, 11, 14

March   1, 9, 14, 16, 17, 20, 23, 29

April   4, 5, 6, 10, 11, 12, 13, 17, 25, 26

May   2, 3, 7, 8, 9, 10, 11, 14, 15, 16, 17, 22, 23, 24, 31

June   3, 5, 12, 18, 19, 26, 27

July   4, 7, 8, 9, 10, 16, 23, 28, 29, 30, 31

August   3, 4, 5, 6, 7, 13, 20, 21, 24, 25, 26, 27, 28, 31

September 2, 17, 21, 28, 29

October	13, 14, 15, 18, 19, 21, 25, 26, 27, 28
November	2, 3, 9, 11, 14, 15, 16, 17, 21, 24, 29
December	7, 12, 13, 14, 15, 18, 19, 20, 22, 26, 27, 28, 29

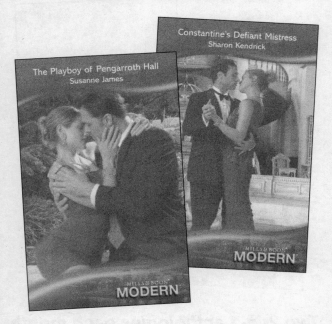

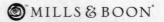